TAKING GOD SERIOUSLY

Vital Things We Need To Know

J. I. PACKER

INTER-VARSITY PRESS
Norton Street, Nottingham NG7 3HR, England
Email: ivp@ivpbooks.com
Website: www.ivpbooks.com

First published 2013

British Library Cataloguing in Publication Data
A catalogue record for this book is available from the British Library.

ISBN: 978–1–84474–609–5

Typeset in the United States of America
Printed and bound in Great Britain by Ashford Colour Press Ltd, Gosport,
Hampshire

CONTENTS

TAKING GOD
SERIOUSLY

PREFACE

We in the West are a very food-conscious lot, and no wonder. Commercials on TV, ads in the newspapers and magazines, roadside billboards, flyers flowing from food stores, sections of magazines, and indeed entire magazines wholly devoted to diet and cuisine keep the allure and joy of eating vividly before our minds. Restaurants parade their styles and specialties all around us, fast-food outlets and coffee shops abound, and supermarkets stocking abundance of shining edibles vie for our custom. No surprise, then, that we over-stock and end up throwing away food that is uneaten or gone bad. No surprise, either, that we overeat and that obesity brought on by imprudent snacking has become a major present-day problem. Food supply is not among our difficulties.

But it is not like that everywhere.

Something approaching a third of the world's population, two billion plus, are undernourished and go chronically hungry since where they live food is regularly in short supply. So do these hungry people always feel hungry? Actually, no; not only does absorption in other things keep hunger at bay for hours, as we all know by experience, but it is unhappily possible to get used to never having enough so that the body settles for always being below par. Then energy evaporates, appetites wither, and lethargy sets in. Famine, which we have all seen on TV, if not in the flesh, produces dull eyes, set features, slow motion, and slow speech. Vitality is absent. People go on living, but their famine-fed apathy shows what they are losing for lack of food. They need adequate regular meals, and need them urgently, which is why the civilized world gives high priority to famine relief.

Nor is famine the only cause of dehumanizing undernourishment.

Extended periods of unbalanced diet—lacking protein, for instance, and short in its calorie count—can yield the same effects. And anorexia becomes self-starvation. Thus, living in the midst of plenty, one still can waste away. Tragic? Yes, but true, as many among us know.

UNDERNOURISHED BELIEVERS

These thoughts illustrate the perspective from which I write this book. As the years go by, I am increasingly burdened by the sense that the more conservative church people in the West, Protestant and Roman Catholic alike, are, if not starving, at least grievously undernourished for lack of a particular pastoral ministry that was a staple item in the church life of the first Christian centuries and also of the Reformation and Counter-Reformation era in Western Europe, but has largely fallen out of use in recent days. That ministry is called *catechesis*. It consists of intentional, orderly instruction in the truths that Christians are called to live by, linked with equally intentional and orderly instruction on how they are to do this.

A VITAL DISCIPLINE FOR ALL CHURCH PEOPLE

There are different levels of catechizing, according to the age groups involved: catechizing is, or should be, a vital ongoing discipline for church people from nine to ninety, so angles, styles, and emphases will naturally vary. There are different ways of catechizing—question and answer, one-on-one; set presentation, orally or on paper, leading to monitored group discussion; offering formulae for memorization and affirmations for amplification; or the time-honored school system of chalk, walk, and talk in didactic dialogue with a class of learners—but essentially the same thing is being done each time. The Bible calls it, quite simply, teaching; on that basis we may further label it, discipling.

Though Bible-based, catechesis is not exactly Bible study, and though it spurs devotion to the Father, the Son, and the Holy Spirit, it is in itself a discipline of thought in God's presence rather than of direct address to the Holy Three, or to any one of them. Its intended end product is Christians who know their faith, can explain it to enquirers and sustain it against skeptics, and can put it to work in evangelism, church fellowship, and the many forms of service to God and man for which circumstances call. As a nurturing discipline, catechesis may be said to correspond to the innermost ring of the dartboard, or rifle or archery target. Bible study meetings and prayer gatherings will reach the outer rings, but it is catechesis—this ongoing procedure of teaching and discipling—that hits the bull's-eye. The fact that all-age catechesis has fallen out of the curriculum of most churches today is thus a major loss, which, as was indicated above, has left many Christians undernourished and hence spiritually sluggish.

CHRISTIAN TRUTH AND APPLICATION

The essence of catechetical material is that it links the formulation of Christian truth (i.e., orthodoxy) with its application in Christian living (i.e., obedience, or orthopraxy, as nowadays it is often called). Several of the New Testament pastoral letters are classic examples. Glance with me at two of them, Paul's epistle to Christians at Rome and the anonymous epistle to Hebrews, that is, to members of Jewish Christian congregations. Both these documents are (1) *kerygmatic*, that is, proclaiming salvation through Jesus Christ, and (2) *didactic*, logically arranged to offer a single flow of foundational thinking. Thus they are (3) *catechetical*, that is, showing how *right belief* requires *right living* through an active faith that responds to Christ crucified, risen, and enthroned, and that likewise responds to all that is and will be ours in and through him, and to the plans of God the Father that undergird this salvation and this hope. (Colossians, Ephesians, and 1 Peter have the same catechetical character, but we cannot look at them here.) The catechetical agenda of Romans and Hebrews becomes clear as soon as we note what doctrinal substance they contain and what impact on the readers addressed is intended.

Though the *readerships* of Romans and Hebrews were differ-ent (Romans was written mainly to non-Jewish converts; Hebrews, mainly to Jewish believers), and though the *styles* of the two writers are different and the situations of the two reading audiences dif-fered, still we find that the following essential, basic *teachings* are set forth in both Romans and Hebrews in complementary ways.

TWO POSITIVE POINTS

1. THE REVELATION OF GOD IN AND THROUGH JESUS CHRIST, THE BRINGER OF SALVATION, OF WHOM BOTH WRITERS ARE SPEAKING WITH AUTHORITY

Jesus Christ is the Son of God, a distinct divine person within the divine unity, to be worshipped as the Father is worshipped (Rom. 1:4; 9:5; Heb. 1:1–14).

Jesus Christ is the Son of God incarnate, a fully divine person in his humanity, whom the Father in love has sent into this world for sinners' salvation (Rom. 1:3–7; 16:25–27; Heb. 2:5–18).

Jesus Christ gave his life at the Father's will as an atoning sacri-fice for sins. He was raised from the dead by the power of God and lives, rules, and will one day return for the final judgment and the completing of our salvation from all sin and evil. Through Jesus Christ as Mediator sinful humans are reconciled to God, justified and forgiven by him, and given permanent access to him. Through Christ's outreach to them they are adopted into God's family, made his heirs with Christ, and assured of his eternal love for them (Rom. 2:5–16; 3:21–5:21; 8:15–23, 31–39; Heb. 2:10–18; 8:1–10:23; 12:5–11, 22–24).

Jesus Christ is the enthroned Lord whom Christians are to wor-ship, call on, trust for help, and serve throughout their lives (Rom. 10:8–13; 13:14; 14:17–18; Heb. 4:14–16; 12:1–3; 13:7–15).

Jesus Christ imparts his own resurrection life to believers through their faith-union with him. This ongoing transformation of them toward full Christlikeness of perception and practice is effected by the Holy Spirit and is expressed in baptism (Rom. 6:1–7:6; Heb. 8:10–12; 10:16–17).

2. THE RESPONSE REQUIRED FROM SINNERS WHO BECOME RECIPIENTS OF SALVATION, TO WHOM BOTH WRITERS ARE ADDRESSING PASTORAL GUIDANCE

Faith is required. *Faith* is a New Testament technical term. It means wholehearted acceptance of, trust in, and obedience to God, branched out into a threefold object: the Word of God, that is, the teaching of the Old Testament and the apostolic writers as such; the promises of God categorically; and the Son of God personally. Faith is credence plus commitment, assurance plus allegiance, and devotion plus discipleship. Faith flows from *understanding* the gospel, which is the effect of *learning* it, which is the outcome of being *taught* it (Rom. 1:16–17; 4:1–5:11; 10:5–17; 14:1–4, 20–23; Heb. 2:1–4; 3:1–6; 4:14–16; 5:11–6:12; 10:19–12:2).

Repentance is required. Repentance, a function of faith, is a remorseful reversing of one's previous self-centered, sin-serving habits and actions and turning to Christ to become his faithful and obedient follower, practicing repentance and pursuing holiness as a lifelong project (Rom. 2:4; 6:12–23; 13:12–14; Heb. 6:1–6; 12:1–4, 14–17).

Hope, motivating *endurance*, is required. Both are functions of faith in action. Hope is the divinely guaranteed certainty of good things to come; endurance is holding fast to one's God-given hope in the face of temptations and urgings to abandon it (Rom. 5:1–5; 8:23–25; 15:4–13; Heb. 3:6; 6:11–20; 10:23; 11:13–16).

Love is required. God, fellow-believers, and one's neighbors generally, are love's objects. Love to God means gratitude for his grace and a devoted doing of his will so as to please him. Love to fellow-believers means welcoming them into, and maintaining their welcome within, the circle of Christian fellowship, there serving their needs, spiritual and physical, encouraging them in their discipleship, and taking care not to thoughtlessly put roadblocks in their path. Love to neighbors as such, whoever they are, means kindness, helpfulness, doing good to them, sharing resources with them, and forgoing all forms of revenge and tit for tat all along the line (Rom. 8:28; 12:6–13; 13:8–10; 14:13–22; Heb. 10:24–25; 13:1–5, 15–16).

THE BUILDING BLOCKS OF GOD'S CHURCH

These positive points are the catechetical basics that these two epistles yield for discipling individual believers, the human building blocks of God's church. Catechetical instruction on the church and church life, Bible-based like the basics listed above, would be the next stage in the discipling process (for which, it may be suggested, Paul's letters to the Ephesians, to Timothy, and to Titus would be the primary New Testament resources).

It should be noted that in Romans and Hebrews the positive points that I have highlighted as, so to speak, the marrow of the discipling message were mostly laid out in what were implicitly, if not explicitly, corrective contexts—where error, inadequacy, and misconception were being exposed in order to be excluded. Clearing the ground mentally, in terms of "not that but this," is in fact part of the catechetical process itself. Educators know that as white looks whiter on a blackboard and black looks blacker on a whiteboard, so meaning is more clearly and sharply seen when contrasted with what is not meant. So, too, competent catechesis (teaching and discipling), like the teaching of the Bible itself, needs to specify negative as well as positive corollaries to achieve fullest clarity in both comprehension and application.

SPIRITUAL NOURISHMENT FOR
ALL CHRISTIAN BELIEVERS

The job of a preface, as I understand it, is to give readers a preliminary word about the book itself by indicating its aim and scope, and, if I may put it so, its wavelength. I hope the preceding pages have done this for the present volume. The chapters included in the book are ventures in adult catechesis, furnishing the mind and forming the judgment regarding key truths that are often challenged today. Since they were first produced separately, and at four-month intervals, some repetition was unavoidable; I ask that it be forgiven, now that they are all together.

As an Anglican, I write with a sense of urgency in response to recent trends in my own church context. But readers who are not Anglicans will recognize many of the same trends in their own denominational circles, and may find that this book speaks pointedly to their situations, challenges, and concerns. So while I write in hope of helping fellow-Anglicans into a mature faith, there is nothing exclusive about this need or aim. I offer examples from my Anglican experience, but before I am an Anglican I am an evangelical, and I have tried to write in such a way that all evangelicals—and would-be and should-be evangelicals—will benefit. The questions after each chapter have an Anglican slant, but I do not think that Christians anywhere who take their Christian commitment seriously will find these questions unfruitful for meditation and discussion in their own neck of the denominational woods.

Thus my prayer is that God may use this material (1) to ground thoughtful Christians more firmly and clearheadedly in their faith, (2) to stir them out of the sluggishness into which theological and spiritual undernourishment has brought so many of us, and (3) to help us all take to heart the marching orders given us by our Lord and his apostles—who charge us first to be and then to make disciples everywhere, starting from where we are. This is the Christian's serious business; God make us serious in attending to it.

1

TAKING FAITH
SERIOUSLY

When a person falls into convulsions, short-term remedies may for the moment calm him down, but the long-term need is to diagnose the root cause of his trouble and treat that. So it is today with churches round the world, including the worldwide Anglican Communion, a body that is over seventy million strong and growing by leaps and bounds in both Asia and Africa. A much-publicized Episcopal decision in Canada to bless same-sex unions as if they were marriages, as well as the consecrating in the United States of a diocesan bishop who unashamedly lives in such a union, has convulsed global Anglicanism in the way that pebbles thrown into a pond send ripples over the entire surface of the water. Pressure groups and leadership blocs have emerged in Anglicanism's "Old West" (Britain, North America, Australasia) resolved to fight this issue till approval of gay pairings is fully established. Tensions over the question between and within provinces, dioceses, and congregations have become acute, and there is no end in sight.

What, we ask, is the root cause of these convulsions? What would be needed to get us beyond them? The fact we must face is that the clash of views on how, pastorally, to view and help male and female homosexuals grows out of a more basic cleavage about faith. To map this and suggest what to do about it is our present task.

WHAT IS FAITH? A WORD THAT SLIPS AND SLIDES

Getting the hang of current disagreements about faith is not easy, for the word *faith* itself is used elusively and does in truth mean different things to different people, though this fact often goes unrecognized. The way of the "Old West" churches, in prayers, sermons, books, and discussions that seek to be unitive, is constantly to refer to the faith as a common property held by all who worship, but without defining or analyzing its substance, so that worshippers can go for years without any clear notion of what their church stands for. Theologians rise up to affirm that, in idea at least, faith goes beyond mere orthodoxy (belief of truth) to orthopraxy (living out that truth in worship and service, love to God and man)—and in saying this they are right so far. But when some think orthodoxy sanctions behavior that others see orthodoxy as ruling out, it is clear that agreement about the truth we live by is lacking, and that is what we have to look at now.

Complicating our task is the fact that all varieties of the dimension of life we call religion (Muslim, Hindu, Buddhist, Jewish, Baha'i, Voodoo, Sikh, New Age, Scientology, and the rest) are regularly lumped together with all the versions of Christianity (Roman Catholic, Orthodox, conservative Protestant, liberal Protestant) as so many *faiths*. This usage makes it seem that all religions should be seen as essentially similar—which is probably how most post-Christian Westerners do in fact see them, though in the church this is very much a minority idea. Then, too, we use the word *faith* for whatever hopes about the future individuals cherish and live by (e.g., that science will save the planet from ruin; that there will not be another economic crash like 1929; that this or that missing person will be found alive; that this or that cancer can be beaten; that every cloud will have a silver lining; and so on). These broader uses of the word grew up as its former Christian precision dissolved away, so that in modern Western speech *faith* has become a vague term, a warm fuzzy slipping and sliding from one area of meaning to another all the time. In the New Testament, however, *faith* is a Christian technical term, specific in meaning as our secular technical terms (*computer, dividend, airplane, spanner, appendectomy, syllabus*, for example) are specific in meaning, and its New Testament meaning remained specific for Christians till about a century ago. It is something we need to get back to.

What did the apostolic writers have in mind when they spoke of faith? Nothing less than what they took to be the distinctive essence of Christianity: namely, a belief-and-behavior commitment to Jesus Christ, the divine-human Lord, who came to earth, died for sins, rose from death, returned to heaven, reigns now over the cosmos as his Father's nominated vice-regent, and will reappear to judge everyone and to take his own people into glory, where they will be with him in unimaginable joy forever. This was "the faith" that was taught and defended against Gnostic syncretists from the start (we see Paul in Colossians and John in his letters actually doing that); soon it was enshrined in creeds, which began as syllabi for catechetical instruction of enquirers; and, with its Trinitarian implications made explicit, it has since then been at the heart of mainstream Christianity everywhere. (The Reformers debated with Roman Catholics as to whether faith brings present justification directly, but no one in the debate doubted that real faith includes all that we have described.)

So faith, that is, believing, is in the New Testament a "two-tone" reality, a response to God's self-revelation in Christ that is both intellectual and relational. Mere credence—assent, that is, to "the faith"—is not faith, nor is commitment to a God or a Christ who is merely a product of human imagination. Christian faith is shaped, and its nature is determined, entirely by its object, just as the impression on a seal is shaped entirely by a die-stamp that is pressed down on the hot wax. The object of Christian faith, as the apostolic writers, the creeds, and the basic Anglican formularies (Articles, Prayer

Book, and Homilies) present it, is threefold: first, God the Three-in-One, the Creator-become-Redeemer, who throughout history has been, and still is, transforming sinners into a new humanity in Christ; second, Jesus Christ himself, God incarnate and Savior, now absent from us in the flesh but personally and powerfully present with us through the Holy Spirit; and third, the many invitations, promises, commands, and assurances that the Father and the Son extend to all who will receive Jesus as their Savior and Lord and become his disciples, living henceforth by his teaching in his fellowship under his authority.

All of this is laid before us in the Bible, the revelatory book that God has given us for the forming of our faith. In the Bible, faith is a matter of knowing the facts of the gospel (the person, place, and work of Jesus Christ), welcoming the terms of the gospel (salvation from sin and a new life with God), and receiving the Christ of the gospel (setting oneself to live as his follower by self-denial, cross-bearing, and sacrificial service). Believing the biblically revealed facts and truths about God and trusting the living Lord to whom these facts and truths lead us are the two "tones," the intellectual and relational aspects of real faith, blending like two-part harmony in music. This is the understanding of faith that needs to be reestablished.

We noted above that in our time the word *faith* has become a warm fuzzy, slipping and sliding in use in and out of its Christian meaning to refer to other modes of believing and behaving that, whatever else they are, differ in significant ways from what we have described. This fuzzification of faith has developed in parallel to increasing ignorance of biblical teaching and growing skepticism as to whether that teaching as it stands may properly be called the Word of God. Is there a connection? Yes. When the church ceases to treat the Bible as a final standard of spiritual truth and wisdom, it is going to wobble between maintaining its tradition in a changing world and adapting to that world, and as the wobbles go on, uncertainty as to what is the real substance of faith and the proper way of embracing it and living it out will inevitably increase.

But the Bible is currently interpreted in many different ways, and scholars' arguments about its meaning are regularly over ordinary people's heads. So even when Scripture is acknowledged as the standard, are confusion and uncertainty likely to be any less? This is a fair question, and to answer it we need to take a longer, harder look at the Bible than perhaps we have ever done before.

WHAT IS THE BIBLE? FAITH AND THE TALKING BOOK

Most people in churches nowadays have never read through the Bible even once; the older Christian habit of reading it from start to finish as a devotional discipline has virtually vanished. So in describing the Bible we start from scratch, assuming no prior knowledge.

The Bible consists of sixty-six separate pieces of writing, composed over something like a millennium and a half. The last twenty-seven of them were written in a single generation: they comprise four narratives about Jesus called Gospels, an account of Christianity's earliest days called the Acts of the Apostles, twenty-one pastoral letters from teachers with authority, and a final admonition to churches from the Lord Jesus himself, given partly by dictation and partly by vision. All these books speak of human life being supernaturally renovated through, in, with, under, from, and for the once crucified, now glorified Son of God, who fills each writer's horizon, receives his worship, and determines his mind-set at every point.

Through the books of the Bible runs the claim that this Jesus fulfills promises, patterns, and premonitions of blessings to come that are embodied in the thirty-nine pre-Christian books. These are of four main types: *history* books, telling how God called and sought to educate the Jewish people—Abraham's family—to worship, serve, and enjoy him, and to be ready to welcome Jesus Christ when he appeared; *prophetic* books, recording oracular sermons from God conveyed by human messengers expressing threats, hopes, and calls to faithfulness; *poetry* books, containing songs to and about God (Psalms) and celebrating love between a man and a woman (Song of Solomon); and *wisdom* books, which in response to God's revelation show how to praise, pray, live, love, and cope with whatever may happen.

Christians name these two collections the Old and New Testaments respectively. *Testament* means covenant commitment, and the Christian idea, learned from Paul, from the writer to the Hebrews, and from Jesus himself, is that God's covenant commitment to his own people has had two editions. The first edition extended from Abraham to Christ; it was marked throughout by temporary features and many limitations, not unlike a nonpermanent shanty built of wood on massive concrete foundations. The second edition extends from Christ's first coming to his return and is the grand full-scale edifice for which the foundations were originally laid. The writer to the Hebrews, following Jeremiah's prophecy, calls this second superstructure the new covenant and explains that through Christ, who is truly its heart, it provides a better priesthood, sacrifice, place of worship, range of promises, and hope for the future than were known under its predecessor. Christians see Christ as the true center of reference in both Testaments, the Old always looking and pointing forward to him and the New proclaiming his past coming, his present life and ministry in and from heaven, and his future destiny at his return; and they hold that this is the key to true biblical interpretation. Christians have maintained this since Christianity began.

Christians call the Bible the Word of God—"God's Word written," as Anglican Article 20 puts it—for two reasons. The first is its divine origin. Jesus and his apostles always treat Scripture as the utterance of God through the Holy Spirit, transmitted by the agency of men whose minds God moved in such a way that in all their composing they wrote just what he wanted as their contribution to the text and texture of the full Bible that he planned. The Bible's quality of being thus completely shaped by God, so that it may and must always be read as God testifying to himself through the testimony to him of the human writers, is its *inspiration*. The second reason for calling the Bible God's Word is its divine ministry of revealing God's mind to us as the Holy Spirit gives understanding of what its text says, and thus makes us "wise for salvation through faith in Christ Jesus" (see 2 Tim. 3:14–17). This quality of thus communicating knowledge of God, of his grace, and of his Son, is the Bible's *instrumentality*. Your word is formally the utterance that proceeds from your mouth and substantially the expression and communication of your mind, and so it is with Scripture as the Word of God: formally, more than a million words strung together; substantially, God's inexhaustible, Christ-centered, salvation-oriented, self-revelation to us. The Bible is both God-given and God-giving, and as such it stands as the standard of Christian faith.

Christianity expresses the thought of Scripture as the standard by calling it the *canon*. This is a Greek word, meaning a measuring rod, and thus a rule. Some have wondered whether the sixty-six-book Protestant canon includes all it should, or contains items that should not be there, but uncertainty about this is unwarranted. There is no good reason for doubting (1) that our Old Testament canon was established in Palestine before Jesus was born, and (2) that the first churches were right to see documents authored and/or approved by apostles as carrying God's authority and complementing the Old Testament, and (3) that they were also right to claim the Old Testament as Christian Scripture and to interpret it as foreshadowing Jesus Christ the Messiah, and the kingdom of God and the new life that came with him.

Nor is there any good reason to fear that the church made mistakes when in the second and third centuries, confronted with spurious gospels, epistles, and acts bearing apostolic names, it identified the genuine apostolic writings and dismissed the rest. Nor do there exist outside the canon any documents that for any reason seem to merit inclusion. At the Counter-Reformational Council of Trent the Roman Catholic Church defined into the canon the twelve-book pre-Christian Apocrypha that Jerome had found in the Greek version of the Old Testament (the Septuagint) and included in his Latin rendering (the Vulgate) in the fifth century; but since these books never belonged to the Hebrew Palestinian canon that Jesus knew, the council's decision must be judged a mistake. It is precisely the books listed in Anglican Article 6 and found in every printed Bible, neither more nor less, that together form the canonical Word of God.

All God's people agree that as God's Word, the Bible has authority—God's authority! What this means is not always clearly seen, but the mainstream understanding is as follows: Authority means the right, and so the claim, to control. Sometimes it operates by agreement, as when authority is given to political leaders, army officers, team captains, and policemen, but in this case it is intrinsic. God has authority because he is God, and we should bow to his authority because we are his creatures. What comes through to humble and openhearted people as they read and study the Bible, or hear it read and taught, is awareness of God's reality as our almighty, morally perfect, and totally awesome Maker, plus the sense that he is telling us truth about relations between him and us, plus a realization that he is calling for, indeed commanding, faith in him and faithfulness to him, repentance and redirection, self-denial and obedience as the path to the life he wants us to taste here and enjoy hereafter. All of this centers constantly on words and deeds of Jesus, the church's living Lord and, as we have said, Scripture's point of reference, who is felt again and again to be stepping out of the book into our lives in order to take them over and change them. The Bible is thus experienced as a book that talks, speaking for itself by pointing us to the Father and the Son, who speak for themselves as they offer us forgiveness and acceptance and new life. The authority of Scripture is not just a matter of God putting our minds straight, but of God capturing our hearts for fully committed discipleship to the Lord Jesus. So the Bible is to be approached with reverence, handled with care and prayer, and studied, not to satisfy curiosity in any of its forms, but to deepen responsive fellowship with God who made us, loves us, seeks us out, and offers us pardon, peace, and power for righteousness through Jesus Christ our Lord.

The modern world knows virtually nothing of this approach to Scripture. It is vital that the church recover it, follow it, and proclaim the need for it everywhere.

For two centuries now in Protestant communities the Bible, like so many more premodern things, has been under suspicion—in this case, of being factually false, spiritually wrongheaded, ethically irrelevant, and antihuman in its overall influence. Once, most Westerners knew something of what was in the "Good Book" to guide us in our lives; nowadays, however, very few know or care what the Bible teaches. Neither at home nor at school is the Bible taught, and it has to be said that church Sunday schools, though strong on favorite Bible stories, often fail to acquaint children with the Bible as a whole. Though the criticisms and doubts about Scripture have been compellingly countered over and over again, that does not change the secular mind-set of our culture or banish biblical illiteracy from our midst. Yet ignorance of the Bible remains tragic, for it virtually guarantees ignorance of God. To reestablish in people's minds the truth and wisdom of the biblical message, so that they see they need to know what is in the Bible in order to enjoy a positive relationship with God, is perhaps the church's most urgent task today.

WHO'S THERE? FAITH AND THE TRIUNE GOD

We saw that taking faith seriously means taking seriously the fact that Christianity has a given and abiding truth-content, and that therefore we must take the Bible seriously as the authoritative, self-revealing Word of our authoritative God. From this it follows that we must take God seriously in the terms in which the Bible displays him. Now we must see what this involves.

A latter-day theological student, we are told, secured an *A* for answering the rather pompous exam question "What is the significance of Jesus Christ for our postmodern era?" in three words— "Whatever you wish." That catches exactly the way people today think and speak of God: the word *God* becomes a wax nose that can be shaped or, rather, twisted out of shape any way one fancies. But fancy is fantasy, and what we need to know is the truth about the God who is there, whom we must all meet on judgment day, and who meets us here and now when we allow the Bible to speak to us. Here is a thumbnail sketch of what the Bible tells us about him.

First, God is *holy*, different and standing apart from us, awesome and sometimes becoming fearsome to us. Holiness is a biblical technical term signifying the God-ness of God, the combined quality of being infinite and eternal; omnipotent, omnipresent, and omniscient; utterly pure and just; utterly faithful to his own purposes and promises; morally perfect in all his relationships; and marvelously merciful to persons meriting the opposite of mercy. God in his holiness is greatly to be praised and worshiped for both his greatness and his goodness at all times. Many of the psalms express this.

Second, God is *gracious*. *Grace* is a New Testament technical term meaning love to the unlovely and seemingly unlovable, love that is primarily not a passion evoked by something in the loved one, but a purpose of making the loved one great and glad: love that to this end gives, never mind the cost, and rescues those in need, never mind their unworthiness. The New Testament focuses throughout on a plan of grace whereby God has redeemed and is now fashioning for endless joy with himself a new humanity, whose members are drawn from a human race—our human race—that is at present ruined and lost.

Third, God is *triune*. *Trinity*, the church's word for expressing this internal three-in-oneness, or triunity, is a technical term
coined to crystallize something that the Bible demonstrates.
Both Testaments affirm that there is only one God, but the New
Testament clearly shows us three divine persons acting as a team
to carry through the work of grace that saves sinners and creates
the church. The first is the Father, who planned everything, who
sent his Son to take human nature and die on the cross in his people's place, thus releasing them from the judgment that faced them,
and who now justifies (that is, pardons and accepts) them, adopt-
ing them as his family and heirs when they put faith in Jesus. The
second is Jesus the Son, God incarnate, his Father's servant, our
Mediator, who died for us, rose for us, reigns for us, and will return
for us—the Savior and Lord whose devoted disciples we are called
to be, and whom we shall be adoring forever. The third is the Holy
Spirit, the executive, hands-on agent of the Father and the Son in
creation, providence, and grace, who draws us to faith in Christ
by making us see that we need him and calls us to come to him,
who unites us to him as we receive him, who renews us constantly
through Word and sacrament, prayer and fellowship, in our new
life of discipleship to him, and who from within that life gives us
glorious foretastes of heaven's happiness and joy. As the three persons are linked together as sources of blessing, so they are linked as
the focus of praise, prayer, and benediction. The New Testament
writers speak consistently on all of this.

What are we looking at? Not tritheism, a doctrine of three
separate gods cooperating; that would in fact be a form of poly-
theism. Nor is it what has been called modalism, a doctrine of one
person playing three separate roles, like the late Peter Sellers in *Dr.
Strangelove*; that would in fact be a form of unitarianism. No; by
inescapable implication it is a doctrine of the only God as a tri-
personal Three-in-One—Trinitarianism in solution, you might say,
throughout the New Testament, as sugar is in solution when you

have stirred it into your coffee. A reality beyond what our minds can grasp? Yes. (We are only creatures, after all; we should not be surprised to find there is more to our Maker than we can comprehend.) A certainty, evident from the mutual relations that the New Testament reveals between the persons in the divine team? Yes, again. A truth to be affirmed as something that is, even though we do not know how it can be? Exactly. So we settle for it as an authentic apostolic conception, enshrined in and safeguarded by the church's technical Trinitarian vocabulary, and we take care not to lose sight of this truth as we move ahead.

Fourth, God *states ideals for, and sets limits to, human behavior.* His moral law is found in the Ten Commandments and backup Mosaic material, in the Prophets, in Jesus's Sermon on the Mount and other teachings, and in the ethical sections of the New Testament letters. Law in Hebrew is *torah*, a word primarily implying not public legislation but family instruction, given with parental authority, goodwill, and concern for the family's well-being. It is vital to realize that God's law, expressing as it does his holy will and reflecting his holy nature, fits and fulfills humanity as created; it is the Maker's handbook, we might say, for human happiness, and disregard of it not only displeases God but also damages ourselves. God has made us and redeemed us so that we might bear his image, which includes, along with rational and responsible wisdom, moral perfection that matches his own. "You shall be holy," he says, "for I am holy" (1 Pet. 1:15–16, citing Lev. 11:44). This means love and worship with obedience Godward, and love and service with wisdom manward. Pleasing God must always be our goal, and lawless disregard of him, of our fellow-humans, and of the behavioral standards that have been set is always sin, needing repentance if it is to be forgiven. All sin is categorically off limits; doing evil even in a good cause cannot please God. The Bible delineates many behavior patterns that God sees as bad and explicitly forbids.

One restrictive maxim spelled out in both Testaments is that the only right place for gratifying our sexual drive, huge and hungry as it may be, is within monogamous marriage, where mutual sexual pleasure is designed to further both pair bonding and procreation. Homosexual acts are explicitly ruled out. Desires for such acts, like other desires to commit sin, must therefore be resisted in God's strength as strongly as possible. Let it be said that all Christians have lifelong battles with similarly unruly desires in some form, although few such desires are hailed as good and glamorized in the way that homosexual urgings are in today's Western societies, and even in some pockets of today's Anglican and other churches. Certainly, saying no to any mode of inappropriate sexual activity may feel for the moment, to use Jesus's image, like cutting off a hand or a foot, or gouging out an eye—negating, that is, some part of yourself that you feel you cannot live well without. But the way of holiness requires of all of us resolute resistance to a wide range of temptations at point after point in our pilgrimage, and all such resistance gives us in the short term something of this same feeling. C. S. Lewis pictures this by his image, in *The Great Divorce*, of the man with the lizard of lust on his shoulder, endlessly whispering to him that without the lust his life will not be worth living. But letting God have his way with the lizard sets the man unimaginably free. The spiritual battles that homosexuals face are thus not unique to them. We all know how sinful desire will masquerade as a special case for which an exception to a general rule may warrantably be made, just as we know all too well the sense of guilt that weighs us down after we have indulged some craving in a way that in our heart we know was wrong. Pastoral care of homosexuals, as of the rest of us, involves strengthening everyone's power to recognize and resist whatever besetting sins they have.

Such, then, is the God of the Bible, the unchanging God who is always there whatever styles or shifts may mark the culture that surrounds the church. This is the God with whom we all have to deal. In an era like ours, in which Western culture is being constantly reshaped by the rapid mutations of post-Christianity, that must be highlighted and insisted on in our faith and witness. God is the same, Jesus Christ is the same, and essential Christianity is the same as they were in the first century, when the pagan world was turned upside down by the witness of the apostles.

WHAT WENT WRONG? FAITH AND THE MELTDOWN OF BIBLICAL TRUTH

When reason insists on ruling—that is, making original decisions of its own—in the realm of faith, where, as we have seen, God's truth should be received on God's authority via God's authoritative written Word, the results are bleak indeed. In comes relativism, the abolishing of all absolute standards for belief and behavior; in comes skepticism about all long-standing beliefs, as if their age automatically destroys their credibility; in comes pluralism, the confused condition in which we accept incompatibles side by side without full commitment to any of them; in comes agnosticism, the don't-know, can't-be-sure, who-am-I-to-say?, I-give-up, don't-bug-me state of mind. Each of these *isms* is familiar among us today, they creep into churches as well as going on parade outside them, and the church of Christ is sadly enfeebled in consequence.

The process of decline that produced this state of affairs, in which most of Western Protestantism has in fact shared, had two stages. First, from the mid-nineteenth century on, biblical criticism, evolutionary dogma, socialist utopianism, and scientific pragmatism have called into question many aspects of biblical teaching and Christian supernaturalism, so that the whole message about Christ, salvation, and the church has become blurred, and the doctrinal definiteness that has marked the Christian tradition is felt increasingly to be unwarranted and unconvincing. Then, second, since the middle of the twentieth century some teachers have recast biblical narratives to which they have denied factual status (miracle stories, including Jesus's virgin birth, bodily resurrection, and ascension to heaven, in the first instance) as symbolizing aspects of the inner experience of the church and the Christian; they have read biblical law codes as directing us to follow the best existing notions of secular justice; and they have spread the idea that loose spiritualizing in this way is the only proper method of biblical interpretation. The effect, as anyone can see, is to turn Christianity into a historically continuous church-based mysticism of transcendental God-feelings and attitudes of benevolence, none of which depends on any space-time events, and all of which, it seems, might cheerfully continue into the future even if it could be shown that Jesus Christ had never lived and that the gospel of salvation from sin is a mere mirage.

Much of the church today, including the Anglican Church of Canada and the Episcopal Church in the United States, has two religions in its womb—or shall we say in its theological colleges, in the minds and hearts of its clergy, in its publications, and in the mentality of its members. There is the historic faith, which this little book tries to identify, and there is the alternative Christianity that we have just described. The former is spelled out, for example, in the historic Book of Common Prayer and was given constitutional status in Canada by the Solemn Declaration of 1893; the fingerprints of the latter, sanitized somewhat, can be found in the Canadian Book of Alternative Services and the American prayer book of 1979. One recalls Elijah's call for clearheaded choice at Mount Carmel: "How long will you go limping [some translations, "hobbling"] between two different opinions? If the Lord is God, follow him; but if Baal, then follow him" (1 Kings 18:21).

A robust return to the older wisdom about faith's true object is urgently needed if the Anglican Church in particular is ever to impact the surrounding culture again. The same must be said of other churches with Reformation roots, both sides of the border, and elsewhere. All in these communities who take faith seriously should unite to work for this return.

1. Can there be orthopraxy without orthodoxy? If not, why not?
2. How should orthodoxy lead to orthopraxy? Think of examples of how this might or might not happen.
3. How would you explain the nature of faith to a nonchurchgoer?
4. How would you explain the importance of the truth of the Trinity to a nonchurchgoer?
5. What forms of pastoral care and fellowship can help a person to resist besetting temptations?
6. What is required to achieve and maintain Christian faithfulness in matters of morality?
7. Is it ever true that the world has the wisdom and the church must play catch-up? In what respects, if any, is this claim not true?

2

TAKING DOCTRINE SERIOUSLY

We shall proceed by question and answer, and plunge in straight away at the deep end.

THE NATURE OF DOCTRINE

First question: What is doctrine?

Doctrine is the revealed truth of God as defined and taught in the church, by the church, for the church, and for the world.

Our word *doctrine* is from the Latin *doctrina*, which means teaching. The corresponding word in the Greek New Testament is *didachē*, which has the same meaning. The New Testament church appears as a community of learners, some of whom become teachers as well, but all of whom are called to the lifelong task of taking in, digesting, and living out, which includes giving out, the good news of Jesus Christ that the apostles expounded to them. *Disciple* translates a Greek word that means learner; the church is seen as a fellowship of disciples, and any congregation that did not consist of persons laboring to learn more about Christ than they knew as yet would hardly count as a church by New Testament standards.

The New Testament highlights one such congregation, that to which the letter to the Hebrews (Jewish Christians) was written. See how the writer chides them: "You have become dull of hearing. For though by this time you ought to be teachers, you need someone to teach you again the basic principles of the oracles of God. You need milk, not solid food .... solid food is for the mature" (Heb. 5:11–14).

33

The writer sees this as a spiritual issue of prime importance, and his forthrightness about it is striking and sticks in the mind. Let us keep this example of faithful ministry before us as we continue.

Doctrine is taught not only by sermons, catechisms, and instructional talks, not only by printed books and audio-visual devices, but also by worship patterns (liturgies, both written and unwritten; hymns and songs) and by creeds, confessions, and declarations of councils and synods. It is learned by attending to these and buttressing them with personal and group Bible study. By all these means Christians and congregations seek to assimilate, articulate, and apply what the apostles taught the first churches in Christ's name. Faithfulness to this heritage is the mark of sound doctrine—doctrine, that is, that promotes spiritual health. Deviations from the heritage constitute false doctrine, which will at least stunt growth and at worst ruin souls completely. Christian doctrine is thus serious business, as serious as anything with which the church ever deals.

The conscientious teaching and learning of doctrine assumes the divine revelation of its content. Doctrine is not just a bundle of the church's own ideas, thoughts, and dreams about God, but is a declaring of what God himself has shown and told us, inscripturating it in the Bible for all time. Doctrine assumes that God uses his gift to us of language to communicate with us; that he is in fact the primary author of the Bible, its human writers being his empowered agents; and that these writers did their work, first to last, under the guidance of the Holy Spirit.

It is clear historically that the present-day devaluation and neglect of doctrine in the Protestant churches of the West, the Anglican Church prominent among them, is due to so-called liberal thought, which inverts the true relationship between Scripture and secular thinking by letting the latter judge, criticize, and correct the former, rather than vice versa. The original, authentic Christian belief, still sustained in Roman Catholic, Eastern Orthodox, and conservative Protestant circles, is that Holy Scripture is in essence

God testifying to himself via human witnesses and writers. This belief is basic to the concept of doctrine, which is to be formulated, communicated, and defended under the authority of biblical teaching throughout. The trust that doctrine expresses—that is, its account of how things are, and how God knows they are, relationally between us and him—comes to us from (to borrow a phrase beloved of John Calvin the Reformer) God's own holy mouth.

The sum and substance of the church's defined doctrine is the gospel itself, the good news of how our Creator has become our Redeemer through Jesus Christ our Lord. Modern usage tends to shrink the gospel to a threefold declaration, often set forth as an ABC in evangelistic contexts:

- All have sinned and now stand under God's judgment.
- Believe on the Lord Jesus Christ and you will be saved.
- Confess Christ as your Savior and Lord. Commit yourself to lifelong service to him. (Two C's for the price of one.)

But, though this is certainly its applicatory center, the gospel says far more than that. In the New Testament the gospel includes all that is contained in the Apostles' Creed—creation; the incarnating, dying, rising, reigning, and return of the Son; and the ministry of the Holy Spirit generating the holy universal church of forgiven sinners, who no longer fear condemnation but anticipate heaven's eternal joy. The gospel is the full declaration of this gracious saving plan that God is fulfilling in and for his spoiled world, plus the full demonstration of the proper response—faith in Christ and repentance, good works, and love both Godward and manward, with gratitude and joyful hope. In the action of Christ the Redeemer, who died and rose to deal with human sin, and in the action of the Holy Spirit, who prompts the entire response to Christ and the gospel, first to last, God the Father fulfills his purpose of glorifying himself by glorifying his Son—the Holy One who was the channel of all the wisdom and power that went into the creation and that now goes into God's ongoing providence, and who today, in his glorified incarnate life, actively communicates to us the fullness of the grace that renews and saves.

Thus it appears that bound up with the revelation of the gospel, as we indicated in the previous chapter, is the truth of the Trinity. The means whereby God the Father made and now saves each believer turns out to be the ministry of two further divine persons within the divine unity. First and fundamental is the *mediatorial* ministry of the Son. Second and complementing the Son's work is the *animating* ministry of the Holy Spirit, the Lord and giver of life, as the Nicene Creed calls him, who relates to the Father and the Son as the executive agent for his two directors. In the second century, Bishop Irenaeus pictured the Son and the Spirit as God's two hands; it was a happy illustration. What we must grasp is that the one tri-personal God, our God, operates as a team, all three persons within the divine unity working together in full conjunction with each other to carry through a single, huge, mind-blowing plan: namely, to establish a multibillion strong community of redeemed human beings, each one an enormously complex entity in creational terms, within a fully reconstructed cosmos, with Jesus Christ the Mediator at its center for all eternity. To say "Wow!" or something equivalent at this point is the appropriate reaction, for it is far beyond us to conceive or imagine this glorious transformation of our more or less disordered selves, living in our more or less disordered world, which is all we know at present.

All through the New Testament, explicitly in some places and implicitly everywhere else, this understanding of the task and target of the Trinity is in evidence. There is no technical discussion or definition of Trinitarianism as such, but this doctrine of the work of the triune God is as truly there in solution, as we said earlier, as stirred sugar is in coffee or tea. And we cannot set forth the gospel biblically without direct reference to this teamwork of the Father, the Son, and the Spirit, hereby confronting those we address with the triunity of God. Sub- and anti-Trinitarian belief always distorts the gospel.

When the Prayer Book litany leads us to ask God to deliver us "from all false doctrine, heresy and schism," we need to realize that false doctrine regularly starts with twisting the revealed truth about the Three-in-One. This has been the story on the grand scale in the liberal Protestant camp over the past two centuries, in which a basically unitarian view of God has generally been taken for granted. Within this theological frame Jesus Christ is reduced to a God-filled man, the Holy Spirit is reduced to a God-sent energy in the world, and the apostolic gospel is simply not there.

THE NECESSITY OF DOCTRINE

Second question: Who needs doctrine?

You do; I do; we all do. Everybody needs doctrine if he or she is ever to know God. Granted, most people are aware that some sort of Supreme Being exists, but nobody comes to know him relationally without first learning key facts about him—who and what he is and what he has done, is doing, and will do—and for this we need doctrine.

Doctrine is the *map* that guides us on our cross-country journeying through the thousand-odd pages of the Bible, on the one hand, and the complexities of godly living, on the other. Doctrine is the *spectacles* through which we discern the stepping-stones across the rapids and through the swamps that keep our feet on the path of life. Doctrine, indeed, is the *surgical cure* for the natural spiritual blindness that otherwise makes it impossible for us to find where the path of life begins. Doctrine is the *data about the Lord Jesus Christ* that makes faith in him possible. And then doctrine becomes, so to speak, the *cookbook* for life, giving the correct recipe for each venture in belief and behavior.

The eclipse of doctrine among liberal Protestants and those

they have influenced has reflected a somewhat confused notion that following Christ is in fact one form (other religions offer other forms) of everybody's natural and even instinctive religion. Since liberalism from the start has been parasitic on the ongoing heritage of mainstream Christian doctrine and devotion, and since it has always claimed to be on the church's cutting edge, the extent of its drift from doctrine in its revamping of piety has not always been discerned. Liberal spokesmen have been adept at sounding more Christian, convictionally, than they really are, and the orthodox have often failed to see where liberal notions—no Trinity, no virgin birth, no objective atonement, no bodily resurrection and ascension, for starters—would take them. But today's almost total neglect among North American Anglicans of catechesis as an integral part of Christian nurture—catechism-work, that is, teaching the basic doctrines that Christians live by and the basic disciplines for living by them—tells its own story; as does the doctrinally uninstructed condition of very many middle-aged and young attendees at Anglican worship services. To follow where the Roman Catholic Church is already leading and restore catechesis, the serious teaching and learning of the doctrines of the faith, is one of Western Anglicanism's most urgent present-day needs. This is true of other Protestant bodies also.

THE RANGE OF DOCTRINE

Third question: How much ground does basic Christian doctrine cover?

The ground that ought to be covered in catechetical Christian instruction, whatever form it takes (and as an exercise of teaching and learning it can take many forms), is effectively delimited and defined by the range of affirmations on which the Christian churches have formally agreed. On the church, the sacraments, and the specifics of salvation, there is a partial split between the Roman Catholic and Orthodox churches, on the one hand, and the churches of the Reformation and their descendants, on the other, though there is emphatic agreement on the importance of these matters. On the other key doctrines that the people of God have distilled from the Scriptures over the centuries, there has been and is today broad substantial agreement. These doctrines include the Trinity; human fallenness and lostness through sin; Christ's incarnation, atonement, resurrection, ascension, present reign, and future return to judgment; the ministry of the Holy Spirit in personal transformation; present fellowship with Christ through the Spirit's agency; and the unending reality of both heaven and hell. Conservative Christians of the evangelical type maintain these agreements with particular clarity in the doctrinal statements on which their own interdenominational organizations are founded, as Thomas Oden and I showed in our book *One Faith: The Evangelical Consensus* (Downers Grove, IL: InterVarsity, 2004).

To be sure, the Bible itself must always be given the last word on human attempts to expound it and codify its teaching, and as these historical formulations of doctrine were produced under its authority, so it must be allowed to assess their adequacy as coverage of the full-dress apostolic gospel for each new generation. Cultural change over the centuries may make new verbalizings of classic doctrines desirable for purposes of clearer communication and understanding. Thus, for instance, the fourth-century Nicene Creed, which was basic to Reformation orthodoxy, focused the Son's relation to the Father by describing him as "begotten, not made; being of one substance with the Father." But what the creed means here can now be put more clearly for moderns in relational language of a kind that did not exist in either the fourth or the sixteenth century. If we say that the eternal person whom the eternal Father names, directs, honors, and exalts as his own Son lives eternally with, through, and for the Father within the unending unity of a single divine entity and energy, we shall be expressing the same truth. And the likelihood surely is that, though the mystery of this transcendent relationship is not dispelled, people will see from this more clearly what the togetherness of the Father and the Son means for them in their own life of praise, piety, and obedience—that is, in their personal, Christ-centered practice of doxology, devotion, and discipleship.

Drawing, then, on the Bible and the history of church doctrine, and angling the selected material in an arresting, lucid, and practical way for adult believers at this time, a thematic syllabus for a catechetical course of instruction might be set up somewhat as follows:

The Authority of the Bible

The canonical Scriptures are unique, both because they tell God's story from creation in the past to consummation in the future and because they have a double authorship throughout: as all the books are in their different ways human witness to God, so just as truly they are also God's witness to himself, given in and through what his chosen penmen said about him. This is what the *inspiration* (that is, the God-givenness) of the books really signifies. Accordingly, the sum and substance of their teaching is to be rated as revealed truth for all time. God does not change, and the books, products as they are, humanly speaking, of bygone cultures, are thus trans-cultural in their authority. Believing and obeying God's Word has always been the foundational frame of godliness; so conforming to the Bible is always the church's calling and task, and every Christian's calling and task too. God's authority in and through the revealed truth of the Bible must ever control and shape our belief and behavior. As for interpretation, the Bible is not in code and is not by and large obscure; the books were written to be understood as they point their readers to God, and they yield up their meaning to all who are prepared to be so pointed. Interpretation should, however, always be a quest for the fullness and coherence of the biblical message, and a rule that must always be observed is that none may "so expound one place of Scripture, that it be repugnant to another" (Anglican Article 20).

The Reality of the Trinity

During Old Testament times the Creator, known to Israel as Yahweh, constantly insisted through his prophets and psalmists that he was the only real God. On this basis, in New Testament times, through the work of Christ and the Spirit, he revealed himself as the tripersonal team of which we spoke earlier. Augustine, the classic Latin-writing theologian of the Western church, thought and taught about God as the One who also was truly Three; classic Eastern Greek-writing theologians Basil of Caesarea, Gregory of Nyssa, and Gregory of Nazianzus—the so-called Cappadocian Fathers—thought and taught about God as the Three who were also truly One. Both approaches harmonize equally with Scripture, and Christians should acknowledge and deploy both. God is the *he* who is *they*. How this is so is a mystery. But that it is so is a biblical fact. As was said earlier, God always operates in his (or their!) unity, that is, as a team, and to bear this in mind when dealing with scriptural passages where only one divine person is mentioned is a thoroughly biblical way to read the Bible.

The Sovereignty of God

The Creator's control over his creation, including rebellious human beings within it, is basic to the biblical view of things. We know we are not robots, but self-determining rational beings, answerable therefore to other people and to God for things we do; yet it remains a fact that as the Father, the Son, and the Holy Spirit sustain us and the world in existence every moment (otherwise nothing and no one would be there), so the triune Lord overrules all that takes place, having himself foreseen and in some real sense foreordained it. All of everybody's freely chosen actions are included in this. Here again is mystery: *how* God can thus overrule is more than we can tell; *that* he does so is biblical fact. Throughout the Bible the knowledge that God is in total control is presented to us as a certainty that is enormously encouraging and supportive. It means that we can totally trust him to fulfill his promises and achieve his purposes, to watch over his own people, keeping them safe through life and carrying them home at last, and to glorify himself by glorifying his Son as Savior and Head of the church, both in its present pilgrimage on earth and in its final heavenly glory. The thought that they are inescapably in God's hands and under his sway makes rebel hearts furious, but brings believers much joy.

The Sinfulness of Humankind

God created our race, and still creates each member of it, in love, but that love is not returned. Instead, the Bible reveals us to ourselves as corporately and individually sinful: that is, disobedient, guilty, defiled (which means dirty), and spiritually helpless before God, not loving him and our neighbors as we should, but self-centered, self-seeking, and self-serving from the bottom of our hearts. Living life on the surface and laboring to keep up appearances as fallen humans do, we are not naturally aware of our own deep-level corruption, but when confronted with the Bible's diagnosis of it, we are not able to deny it. "From within, out of the heart of man, come evil thoughts, sexual immorality, theft, murder, adultery, coveting, wickedness, deceit, sensuality, envy, slander, pride, foolishness. All these evil things come from within, and they defile a person" (Mark 7:21–23). So said the Lord Jesus, divine reader of hearts. And who, having heard the symptoms listed, can claim freedom from the infection? The salvation that we need—that is, the rescue, deliverance, restoration, and reinstatement, with renewed power to love and serve and worship as we are meant to do—is precisely the salvation that God gives in and through Christ to all who will receive it by receiving him. But we shall appreciate it properly only as we grasp the depth and hopelessness of our current plight in sin.

Jesus Christ, Savior and Lord

"God so loved the world, that he gave his only Son, that whoever believes in him should not perish but have eternal life" (John 3:16). "So" means not "so much" but "in the following manner." "Gave" points to the Son's obedient self-humbling to become, without loss of deity, a Galilean teenager's baby, then to accept impoverishment as a peripatetic preacher, and finally to endure immolation on a Roman cross as a sacrifice for human sin. God the Father's wise love made his beloved Son mankind's representative, to bear the just retribution that God's holiness required for mankind's sins, and thus to be our penal substitute, tasting death and indeed hell for us. "Eternal life" is the fellowship with the Father in pardon and peace, love and joy, worship and service, filial freedom and contentment that becomes the believer's destiny, starting now and going on forever. "Believe in" is the two-tone, whole-soul reality of faith, which is both embrace of gospel truth with the mind and trust from the heart in the crucified, risen, living, reigning Jesus to whom that truth points. Jesus is to be acknowledged as both sin-bearing Savior and enthroned Lord, and trusting him entails both repenting of sin and becoming his disciple—a truly life-changing transaction.

In 2 Corinthians 5:21 Paul pictures Christ's ministry to us as essentially a great exchange whereby "he [the Father] made him to be sin who knew no sin [but was counted a sinner representatively, as our substitute, taking our place under condemnation], so that in him [through the solidarity with him that faith effects] we might become the righteousness of God [related to God the Father with full acceptance, as the fully obedient Son is]." In other words, the sin of our graceless lives was laid on Christ, and the righteousness of his obedient life was laid on us: he suffered our retribution, and we go free. This is justification by grace through faith in Christ. The solidarity here requires us to count ourselves dead and risen with him. Paul models this for us. "I have been crucified with Christ. It is no longer I who live, but Christ who lives in me. And the life I now live in the flesh I live by faith in the Son of God, who loved me and gave himself for me" (Gal. 2:20). All real Christians echo that.

The Holy Spirit, Life-giver and Sanctifier

The third person of the Trinity, through whom all true spiritual life from Adam onward has been generated, was given at Pentecost to indwell all Christians as the Spirit of Christ, and in that role to do three new things for them:

1. To witness within their hearts to their ongoing union with the risen Savior, and to their adoption into the Father's family, and to their inheritor status with Christ, who is now their elder brother in that family.
2. To change their character into the moral likeness of Jesus by enabling them to practice the virtues of love, joy, peace, patience, kindness, goodness, faithfulness, gentleness, and self-control (the fruit of the Spirit, according to Gal. 5:22–23). This is their sanctification.
3. To equip them for ministries of word and work that will in truth be Christ himself in them, ministering to his people through his people. Every-member ministry in the church of Christ should be the rule everywhere; all gifts are given to be used, and not to use them is to quench the Spirit.

Christian life is precisely life in the Spirit—worship, service, holiness, and fellowship with Christ, all empowered from on high.

The Church in God's Plan

The New Testament speaks of the church as the people of God, the Father's family, the body of Christ, the fellowship of believers, and the community of the Holy Spirit. Each local congregation really is, and must ever seek to show that it is, the one universal church in miniature, an outcrop, sample, paradigm, and microcosm of the greater reality. The universal church is God's new humanity, an international, multiracial, multicultural society in which the ordinary divisions between human groups are transcended by constant effort to express unity in Christ. The calling out and building up of the universal church to serve the Lord Jesus, its Head, is now God's central concern in this world, and should be ours too. Individual Christians, and small groups of believers, enjoy the fullness of God's love and care—no doubt about that!—but they are not, so to speak, the only pebbles on the beach, and they must never allow themselves to think or feel that they are. All Christians are part of the world church, the community that is already one in Christ, and we all should aim to realize and live out that larger identity.

Preaching and teaching the Bible, ordained administration of the sacraments, worship and prayer together, pastoral care and discipline, mutual service and help, and outreach to the neighborhood and beyond—both evangelistic and need-focused, Good Samaritan style—these activities should be the staple elements of the church's corporate life. The church is a supernatural society living a supernatural life of communion with Christ and fellowship with one another in Christ, and each local congregation must work creatively and hard to manifest this in every appropriate way.

And love, meaning a sustained concern for the well-being of others, must hold it all together.

In many churches, it seems to me, a catechetical course for adults, covering at least the seven topics listed and the themes sketched out on each, and proceeding perhaps at the rate of one topic a week (though some might need two weeks), would be of real benefit. The topics and themes are not as familiar to us as they should be, and doctrinal ignorance or incompetence regarding them will leave us very vulnerable when debate arises, as surely it will.

DOCTRINE AND ETHICS

It is often assumed nowadays that Christian ethics is a freestanding study of perceptions and urges that spontaneously arise in Christian hearts as the law of universal love is internalized. But no—the rules of Christian conduct are ordinarily determined by facts enshrined in doctrines, one way or another. Here are three examples.

The great command to love God and one's neighbor with all one's powers is in the first place a grateful recognition of, and response to, God's love already shown us in creation, providence, and grace; and in the second place it is a call for loyal imitation of God, who made our neighbor in his own image and loves him or her unconditionally on that account.

The prohibition of coveting (tenth commandment) is shaped by the knowledge that what each person has was given by God for his, her, or our good. So we are to be content with what we have and make the best of it, not fret over what someone else has and we haven't, let alone try to grab it from them.

The forbidding of homosexual relations is a spin-off from the doctrine of marriage and the family. The Bible shows us that God created the two genders for heterosexual attraction, with delight, leading to lifelong monogamous marriage for, among other things, the raising of stable and mature families; and he created sex for procreation with pleasure, and for reinforced bonding of the marriage relationship thereby. This is part of the God-given and God-taught order of creation, an order that same-sex unions directly contravene. So, however high-minded the participants and however faithful to each other they intend to be, same-sex bodily unions may not be viewed as a form of holiness (the Canadian Anglican General Synod of 2004 was wrong to speak of their "sanctity"), any more than sex with an animal (bestiality) can be so viewed. God sets limits, and obedience to him includes observing them. Sex is for marriage, and marriage is a heterosexual partnership, whatever modern society may say. In our fallenness we all experience improper desires, if not for homosexual orgasms then for other things, but improper desires must be recognized as such (Scripture will indicate) and then resisted, for the glory of God and the good of our own souls.

These examples show how truly ethics is a doing of the truth that doctrine proclaims. Right living is a matter of behaving in a way that expresses and celebrates Bible truth, not defies it. The standards of right living are set by right doctrine. Christian morality is rooted in reverence for God's revealed truth.

THE ALTERNATIVE TO TAKING DOCTRINE SERIOUSLY: AMBIGUITY AND FOG

I would not have wished to end this chapter on a sad and sour note, but realism seems to require it as an illustration of what happens when doctrine is not taken seriously.

A Canadian journalist, an immigrant like myself, wrote that the great Canadian commandment is, "Thou shalt be ambiguous." This touches not only politicians, the constituency that he had in view, but church leadership too. In England I got tired of being told that ambiguity was Anglicanism's great virtue, and I hoped when I responded to Canada's call that I was leaving all that tommy-rot behind. But no. As one who sees truth and clarity as primary Christian values, and the ambiguity that dodges or fudges issues of truth as harmful to people and dishonoring to God, I found the Anglican Church of Canada intensely saddening.

To illustrate what I mean: the 2007 General Synod bogged itself down in supreme ambiguity when it passed the motion that "the blessing of same-sex unions is not in conflict with the core doctrine (in the sense of being creedal)" of the ACC.

What constitutes the "core" doctrine of the ACC? To say "creedal" solves nothing, for the Patristic creeds claim only to echo the Bible; they are in essence summaries of the framework of Bible-based doctrine in which enquirers into Christianity (catechumens) were being instructed, and they do not deal directly with ethical questions at all. Yet, in that they speak of God as Creator, they may be said to refer implicitly and indirectly to the Bible doctrine of marriage and sex that was stated above. And certainly, in the era that produced the creeds Christians were solid in opposing homosexuality, so that, if anything, the creeds called the Synod's motion into question from the inside, turning it into something of a misstatement and indeed an example of nonsense, and thus implicitly ruling out from the start what the homosexual lobby wanted to bring in.

And the motion was formally ambiguous in another way. What does "not contrary to" imply? If it meant only that the creeds, like the Articles, do not mention homosexuality, then the motion was a trivial one, leaving the debate essentially where it was. But if the implication was that, not being ruled out by the creeds, same-sex blessing must be judged an *adiaphoron*—something that makes no difference to the church's faithfulness or well-being and must therefore be judged an acceptable church practice, never mind how many oppose it—well, in that case the same procedure could justify such things as murder, adultery, torture, bestiality, and what not else in the Christian fellowship. All that would be needed would be a declaration in synod that these things were not contrary to Anglican core doctrine in the sense of creedal; which shows, I think, that there is something wrong with this way of reasoning. (In fact, of course, the motion was intended simply to clear the way for the next motion, formally authorizing the practice of same-sex blessing, which providentially did not pass.)

So where did this leave the Anglican Church? In a fog of confusion—a fog that, it seems, was only thickened by the Synod's performance. The whole story is a cautionary tale about what happens when doctrine is not taken seriously and ambiguity is attempted for political purposes. But we cannot pursue that here.

That all our churches will now learn to take doctrine seriously, for their own good, must be the desire and prayer of us all.

QUESTIONS FOR STUDY AND DISCUSSION

1. How would you define doctrine?
2. Do you agree that teaching and learning doctrine is a necessity for healthy church life?
3. How do you think doctrine should be taught in the church?
4. In your view, is the catechetical syllabus for adults proposed in this chapter (a) too large, (b) too small, or (c) just right?
5. Are you convinced that ethics rests on doctrine, so that its commands and prohibitions are direct responses to biblical facts?
6. Do you agree with this chapter's negative assessment of ACC General Synod 2007's dealing with homosexuality? If not, what do you think should be said about it?

3

TAKING CHRISTIAN
UNITY SERIOUSLY

None of us, I suppose, would choose to live through such ongoing agony as that which plagues the current Anglican Communion. And no Christian, I imagine, who was around thirty years ago ever dreamed that Anglicanism worldwide would ever be in the state it is in today.

There is no secret about what has happened. Because recent Anglican history reflects the breakdown of Christian unity in many quarters of the church, a review of that history can be instructive to us all.

ANGLICAN AGONY ABOUT HOMOSEXUALITY

In the 1960s homosexual behavior was decriminalized in most of the Western world. From this move sprang homosexual politics whereby gays pressed for a goal beyond bare tolerance—namely, equal respect and equal rights with heterosexuals in all departments of society. One branch of homosexual politics was the mounting of pressure on churches for recognition of gays and gay behavior as spiritually healthy, of gay unions as a mode of holiness equivalent to marriage, of the fitness of practicing gays for leadership, and of the wrongness of making overt homosexuality a reason to hold them back from it. Homosexuals in all walks of life were encouraged to "come out" so as to strengthen the case for gay equality, and "gay pride" days began to be held in big cities. In Anglican as in other churches, the cry went up for ordaining practicing gays and opening all ecclesiastical offices to them.

The 1998 Lambeth Conference took a stand with the Roman Catholic and Eastern Orthodox churches, plus two millennia of Christian history, by explicitly affirming that homosexual behavior was contrary to Christianity and could not be approved. But in 2002, in the synod of the diocese of New Westminster, Canada, the bishop accepted a request from a majority of those present to begin the public blessing of same-sex couples, at which nearly a hundred delegates declared their communion with the bishop and synod broken and showed that they meant it by walking out. This was painful, but they saw the bishop's commitment as flying in the face of definitive biblical prohibitions and of the gospel's equally definitive demand for repentance from previous sins, including homosexual behavior (see 1 Cor. 6:9–11); and the maiming of the gospel that the bishop's decision involved left them, as they saw it, with no choice. Their walkout was like a pebble thrown into a pond; the ripples spread, and soon the entire Anglican Communion was involved at both the diocesan and provincial levels. It became apparent that in what I have been calling the Anglican "Old West" (Britain, North America, Australasia) the gay case, viewed as a plea for justice, had already gained a good deal of traction, while to the younger provinces of Asia and Africa homosexual behavior remained absolute anathema, just as it is among those (Muslims particularly) with whom they labor to share the gospel knowledge of Christ. This internal Anglican upheaval reflects and highlights the depth of the cleavage between liberal theology in its manifold manifestations and the historic biblical orthodoxy to which the Anglican Communion is publicly committed, both confessionally and constitutionally. The Communion now faces a possibility of division, and accusations of having disrupted its unity are made from all sides.

OUR AGENDA

That is the lead-in to our present discussion. We shall explore together not the debate that homosexual politics has triggered, but the questions about Christian unity that it has raised. Anglicanism is now divided: who broke its unity? In any case, was the international brotherhood of Anglican provinces in full communion with each other an example of true Christian unity? What is the unity that, in obedience to apostolic teaching and for the fulfillment of Jesus's own prayer, we should now aim to realize and maintain and cherish? We will seek clarity on these and related questions.

THE CALL TO CHRISTIAN UNITY

Our starting point will be a long, hard look at two key New Testament passages on unity. The first, from the Gospels, is John 17:20–23, where Jesus prays for the unity of all his disciples.

> I do not ask for these only [the eleven faithful disciples, for whom Christ has been praying thus far in the chapter], but also for those who will believe in me through their word, that they may all be one, just as you, Father, are in me, and I in you, that they also may be in us, so that the world may believe that you have sent me. The glory that you have given me I have given to them, that they may be one even as we are one, I in them and you in me, that they may become perfectly one, so that the world may know that you sent me and loved them even as you loved me.

"That they may be one even as we are one." In the earlier days of the ecumenical movement, great play was made with this passage as a mandate for seeking church union. What Jesus has in view, however, is clearly not any form of an all-embracing ecclesiastical organization. He is speaking, rather, of a fourfold togetherness that may be spelled out as follows:

First, it is a togetherness of *discerning thought*, a matter of solidarity in perception of and belief in what is real and true. The "glory" that the Father gave to the Son and the Son gave to his disciples (v. 22) is surely God's self-display ("glory" in Scripture often means this) in the revelation of "grace and truth" that Jesus declared and embodied (John 1:14–18), the revelation that through the gospel the Holy Spirit leads the spiritually benighted into knowing and fellowshipping with God. Jesus referred to this when, earlier in his prayer, speaking of the faithful eleven, he said, "I have given them the words that you gave me, and they have received them" (17:8). As, according to Jesus, the Father and the Son think together in the unity of their Trinitarian life, the Father planning all the Son's course of action and the Son identifying with all that the Father intends for him (see John 5:19–23; 8:26–29; 12:49–50), so Christians are to identify with the thoughts and teachings of both the Father and the Son, as these are recorded for us in Scripture. That will mean that Christians think together and see eye to eye with each other regarding God's nature, will, and work, so that a shared *orthodoxy* (right belief, as the word literally means) will take form and be firmly held among them.

Second, this unity is a togetherness of *spiritual life*: togetherness, that is, in what Jesus called "eternal life" and in a meditative moment in his prayer defined as knowing "you the only true God, and Jesus Christ"—myself!—"whom you have sent" (17:3). This means (1) our recognizing the reality of God and the Lord Jesus; (2) our responding to the spiritual impact of the Father and the Son mediated through the apostolic word, just as living things in this world respond to physical stimulation; (3) our undergoing the inner change that Jesus described to Nicodemus as being born again of water and the Spirit (John 3:3–7), whereby Jesus, dying for sins and drawing us to himself, becomes the central focus of our life (3:14–21); and (4) God's imparting of energy to stand against the world and the Devil and to spread the gospel message (17:14–16, 20). This eternal life in its fourfoldness results from Christ himself being in us, united to each one in a way that sustains divine vitality in the human soul and binds us all to each other through the binding of each one to him.

Third, the oneness that Jesus described is a togetherness of *active love*: love that is motivated and animated by knowledge of the redemptive, life-transforming love of God to us (vv. 23, 26). Our love will labor to honor and exalt in every appropriate way everyone who is its object: God, by thankful praise, faithfulness to the revealed Word, and proclaiming the gospel of grace; and our neighbors, by rendering them service and relieving their need in all its forms. It will be holy love, maintaining God's moral standards in all that it does. It will indeed be supernatural love, springing from heart-allegiance to the Lord Jesus, whose saving union with believers—"I in them" (v. 23)—is the necessary means whereby this love comes to be.

Fourth, this unity is a togetherness in *missional ministry*. When the incarnate Son was on earth, the Father and he, the sender and the sent, were, as we would put it nowadays, on mission together, carrying out a work of redemption that would issue in a ministry of grace and salvation to the world. The Son's postresurrection commissioning of his disciples—"As the Father has sent me, even so I am sending you" (John 20:21)—involves all Christians in the mission, one way or another, for as long as we are in this world. We are called to be one, united and cooperating in actively spreading the gospel, in and under Christ as mission leader.

This, then, is the Christian unity—unity, that is, of Christians—for which Jesus prayed: a common loyalty to him first and foremost, expressed in clearheaded adherence to his teaching, wholehearted appreciation of his gift of eternal life, holy love as a style of living, and a primary commitment to the missional task of spreading the gospel worldwide. It is a unity that in principle Jesus had already created between himself and the faithful eleven, as John 17:6–19 shows, and that is now to extend to all believers in every generation. Encountering this unity in action is what will convince the world that, so far from being a revolutionary eccentric whom the authorities did well to get rid of, Jesus Christ was truly sent by God to bring us to God, and that God loves us Christians just as he loves the Christ, his own Son, who has given us new life in himself (v. 23). We note that no form of church organization is mentioned in the text, and we infer from this that organization will be relevant to Christian unity only insofar as it expresses and furthers the given oneness in Christ that we have described.

DIMENSIONS OF CHRISTIAN UNITY

Alongside all this we now set Paul's words in Ephesians 4:1–6.

> I therefore . . . urge you to walk in a manner worthy of the calling to which you have been called, with all humility and gentleness, with patience, bearing with one another in love, eager to maintain the unity of the Spirit in the bond of peace. There is one body and one Spirit—just as you were called to the one hope that belongs to your call—one Lord, one faith, one baptism, one God and Father of all, who is over all and through all and in all.

"Maintain the unity of the Spirit": this is Paul's concern here, and in the passage quoted and the verses that follow he does two things. First, logically, he reminds us of the realities that contribute to, and together constitute, that unity. Second, ranging wide, he indicates how we are to work to maintain it. We look now at both these matters.

First, what is the unity of the Spirit? It is a given reality that results from the involvement of many people not only with the Holy Spirit but also, through the Spirit, with the incarnate Son who is currently, by the Father's appointment, the church's and the world's rightful Lord, and with the Father himself, the eternal Father of the eternal Son, who has become our adoptive Father through Christ (see Rom. 8:14–17; Gal. 4:4–7; 1 John 3:1–2). Christ himself put the Holy Spirit's ministry in focus when he said, "He will glorify me, for he will take what is mine and declare it to you" (John 16:14). And Christ and his glory are central in every aspect of the Spirit's post-Pentecost ministry, whether it be illuminating our minds to understand the person, place, and saving performance of Christ, or generating faith in Christ and uniting us to him in his risen life, or transforming us individually into the moral image of Christ, or bonding the church together in its growth toward corporate maturity in Christ. Should the revealed doctrine of Christ be diminished or distorted, or personal faith, repentance, and discipleship be dissolved into conformist "churchianity," or mutual loving service give way to soulless organized routines or to bitter animosity in conflict and division, or interest in the spiritual advance of individuals and of the church as a whole be lost, then the unity of the Spirit would be radically damaged, and Christ himself deeply dishonored.

Within the Trinitarian frame (one Spirit, one Lord, one Father) Paul mentions four specific realities of unity, each of which casts its own light on the glory of Christ, in and through whom Christians are one.

There is one *faith*. This is basic. Faith is our response of heart, mind, and strength to God's self-presentation to us in grace and mercy. In the broadest sense, it may be said that faith is a belief of, and response to, everything about God that the Bible tells us. But in the narrower, sharp-edged sense in which the New Testament usually speaks of it, faith focuses precisely on two things: on Jesus Christ himself, the living Lord and Savior, who once called himself the truth, meaning the ultimate reality that all must face (John 14:6); and on the truths that the Bible as a whole, and the apostles in particular, set forth regarding him. Faith's double response is then embrace of the truths about Christ and personal trust in him, trust that leads to a break with our former way of living, a life commitment of discipleship to him, and an anchoring of all our deepest hopes in him—which is the next point. Before we move to it, however, we should remind ourselves again that it is through the Holy Spirit's work of illuminating our hearts and minds and interpreting biblical teaching to us that we realize those realities and so are led to faith. There would be no unity of the Spirit without this ministry from the Spirit, making us Christians.

There is one *hope*. When God through the gospel calls us to the feet of Christ in faith and repentance, this hope becomes ours. Paul elsewhere speaks of "Christ Jesus our hope" (1 Tim. 1:1). What does he mean? To answer this question, we must note, first, that we humans are a hoping species. All of us live very much in our personal hopes for the future, and few things so unite people as a shared hope; the history of political revolts and revolutions illustrates this abundantly. And we must note, second, that just as Christianity is a religion based on achievement, namely, Christ's achievement of salvation for us, so Christianity is a religion oriented to hope, a faith that looks forward to what more God has promised to do. Jesus Christ will return; he will then perfect his people through their bodily resurrection, and in a re-created cosmos he will have them with him forever in a joy surpassing anything this life can offer. Writing to the Philippians, Paul personalizes this:

> To me to live is Christ, and to die is gain. . . . To . . . be with Christ . . . is far better. (1:21, 23)

> I have suffered the loss of all things and count them as rubbish, in order that I may gain Christ and be found in him . . . that I may know him and the power of his resurrection . . . . One thing I do: forgetting what lies behind and straining forward to what lies ahead, I press on toward the goal for the prize of the upward call of God in Christ Jesus. (3:8–10, 13–14)

To share this hope and live in the power of it and speak of it often has a wonderfully unifying effect in Christian circles. Here is a further aspect of the unity of the Spirit that would not be, had the Spirit himself not given us inklings and foretastes of our future with Christ and so made us into hopers of Paul's kind.

There is one *baptism*. In the New Testament, the rite of baptism has multiple meanings. It is certainly a badge of one's identity as a disciple of Christ and a pledge of loyalty to him. It is certainly a sign of the washing away of sins through the blood of Christ and an assurance to believers that their sins have indeed been cancelled. And the symbolism of going under water and then coming out, or up, from under signifies the reality of dying with Christ to one's past life and rising in him and with him into a life that is wholly new. (This applies irrespective of how much water one goes under and whether one receives the rite as an adult or as an infant.)

Since each Christian is baptized separately, what does Paul mean when he says there is *one* baptism? Is he just affirming the truth that baptism has the same meaning for everyone who receives it? His flow of thought in context indicates that he is saying more than that. Thinking of baptism in a Christ-centered and Spirit-centered way, he is reminding us that we should see every administration of baptism as Jesus Christ reaching out to embrace the candidate, and as a token of the truth that "in one Spirit we [believers] were all baptized into one body . . . and all were made to drink of one Spirit" (1 Cor. 12:13). Which brings us to the fourth and last of the specifics of unity that Paul is listing here.

There is one *body*. Paul's favorite conception of the organic, Spirit-given and Spirit-driven life of the church of Christ is that it is his body, an image that bulks large in Ephesians (see 1:22–23; 3:6; 5:23–30). The point of the picture is that as the functioning of the human body is a marvelous exhibition of unity in diversity and diversity in unity—diverse body parts in a complex yet coordinated variety of movement, all under the control and direction of a single governing mind—so it should be, Paul urges, in the church. For the church is a great diversity of people with very diverse abilities and skills whom Christ, the church's Head and

Lord, wills should behave, and moves to behave, in a cooperative and complementary way for the upbuilding of the church as such and of all who belong to it.

In this common life of mutual service, just as in faith, hope, and baptism, as we have seen, the acting of the Holy Spirit is fundamental. For it is he who, as he indwells us, gives us our gifts for ministry and who acts to animate and moderate our use of them in mutual love, so that order rather than disorder prevails and edification rather than hurt and damage results. Paul dwells on this in the verses of Ephesians 4 that follow, sharing his vision that we all might

> attain to the unity of the faith and of the knowledge of the Son of God, to mature manhood [Greek, "to a full-grown man"; so ESV margin], to the measure of the stature of the fullness of Christ . . . . Speaking the truth in love, we are to grow up in every way into him who is the head, into Christ, from whom the whole body, joined and held together by every joint with which it is equipped, when each part is working properly, makes the body grow so that it builds itself up in love. (Eph. 4:13, 15–16)

When the Spirit's leading into loving mutual service is followed, as evidently it was at Thessalonica, the church is healthy and strong (see 1 Thess. 4:1–12; 5:8–24); but when it is not followed, as at Corinth, the Spirit's gifting is abused, and permanent immaturity and damage threaten (see 1 Cor. 3:1–4, 10–18; 12–14; 16:13). Keeping in mind the God-given unity and destiny of the universal church will make us work hard to preserve and display its unity at the local level for the glory of Christ, who is its Head, its hope, and its life.

PRINCIPLES OF CHRISTIAN UNITY

In light of the two passages that we have studied, we can now formulate some key principles regarding Christian unity for the guidance of our future thinking.

1. CHRISTIAN UNITY IS BOTH A
PRESENT GIFT AND A FUTURE GOAL

Christian unity is something distinct from both church union and Christian fellowship. Simply and basically, it is the state of being united to, alive in, and governed by, Jesus Christ our living Lord, in company with all other Christians, past and present, those now with Christ in the heavenly Jerusalem of Hebrews 12:22 and those on earth with us today. As each Christian is in Christ and is one with him, so all Christians are one with each other in and through him. "Christian" here means, quite specifically, a believer who is born again, knows Christ, is indwelt by the Spirit, and seeks to live in love to the glory of the triune God. Christian unity is the active, acknowledged togetherness of all Christian people, who share their supernatural life in their Savior's love and who love each other across all boundaries of race, color, social standing, and denominational churchly identity. From this standpoint Christian unity is a divine gift and foretaste of heaven, and is entirely the fruit of God's grace.

From another standpoint, however, Christian unity is a goal not fully reached at this time, by reason of differences of belief and behavior among those who profess faith. Persons in the churches who depart from historic Christian and biblical standards in either department, and teach and lead others to do the same, obstruct, disfigure, and actually disrupt Christian unity, no matter how sincere they may be in thinking they are in the van of theological wisdom and spiritual progress. We cannot read hearts and are not therefore able to tell whether those who lapse this way are Christians in the real sense or not, but we can and must say that their lapses create barriers to our acknowledging of Christian unity with them, for that is indeed the case. Full unity with merely partial believers is not possible.

2. CHRISTIAN UNITY IS BOUNDED BY REVEALED TRUTH

This principle pursues the point just made. What God thinks and says is for Christians the absolute standard of truth. God spoke freely to reveal his mind about the realities of redemption and of redeemed life throughout the entire history of his redemptive work, from the days of Genesis to the days of Christ and his apostles some two millennia ago. That revelation is recorded and embodied in the canonical Scriptures, which the Holy Spirit inspired so as to give the world in every age an accurate knowledge and understanding of what God had said and done. What was thus revealed and recorded now stands over against every human idea and cultural consensus to measure how far they are true or false by the yardstick of God's Word. All who recategorize Holy Scripture as well-meant and religiously insightful but factually unreliable human tradition, and assume the right to pass judgment on its truth and wisdom rather than letting it pass judgment on them, undermine Christian unity rather than advance it, and create huge confusion and vast spiritual uncertainty in the process. Little as controversy should be encouraged or enjoyed, those who would uphold the cause of Christian unity have to make clear the falsity of this intellectual method and its results, and must go on making it clear until (please God) this aberration becomes a thing of the past.

3. EXPRESSING CHRISTIAN UNITY IN HUMAN LIFE REQUIRES A SUBSTANTIAL SHARING OF CHRISTIAN HOPE AND A PRINCIPLED PRACTICE OF CHRISTIAN LOVE

One dimension of biblical Christian unity is its two-world outlook on life and its emphasis on the prospect of future glory—peace, joy, and supreme well-being—with Christ in the heavenly city that God has promised and prepared and that now waits to be revealed when Christ comes again. This future hope is part of the truth in which Christians unite, and their looking forward to it together is itself a bond of union. The New Testament sees Christians as aliens and exiles in this world. Yes, we serve God here and enjoy countless blessings as we do so, but all the time we are on our way (*in via*) through basically hostile territory to unimaginable peace and joy in closeness to our Savior in a world beyond (*in patria*), a world that is our real home. One of the defects of Christianity as it is often set forth today is that this two-world perspective is absent and the focus is entirely on the present order of things, in which nothing is perfect and which we must all leave behind in due course. The yawning gulf between those who cherish and those who obstruct Christian unity becomes very clear when Christian hope comes up for discussion and the prospect of changing this world is set forth in glorious Technicolor, while the prospect of heaven's joy is dismissed as mere escapism. C. S. Lewis was wiser when he pointed out somewhere that it is regularly the most heavenly minded people who are of most earthly use.

Christian love for one another, as an expression of our unity in Christ, must be practiced responsibly, in light of what God has told us in Scripture and shown us in Christ about his ideal standards for human living. Failure to do this will disrupt Christian unity yet again. The idea that loving people—one's children, spouse, friends; disadvantaged and abused groups—means giving them everything they ask for and tolerating whatever they choose to do is a sad, sub-Christian mistake. Love gives, certainly, but giving that does not observe the limits of behavior acceptable to God and that does not, however indirectly, give encouragement and help toward self-control, emotional maturity, courage, humility, patience, truthfulness and trustworthiness, purity and holiness, and Christlikeness generally, is not Christian love in action. Moral insensitivity and indifference cancel Christian love, instead of expressing it. It is not loving, in the Christian sense, to confirm anyone, let alone fellow-Christians, in wrong ways, and it is certainly not the way to acknowledge our Christian unity with anyone. Christian love is unconditional in the sense of accepting, respecting, and showing goodwill to people just as they are, but it is not unconcerned or undiscerning about being beneficent as distinct from merely indulgent. True Christian love holds to Christian standards all the way.

4. PRACTICING CHRISTIAN UNITY IN CONGREGATIONAL LIFE REQUIRES PATIENT EFFORT AND ACTIVE SHARING AT ALL LEVELS

In local congregations, where the reality of corporate life in Christ should be on show and visible to all, the New Testament makes clear that four things at least are called for.

First, *the pursuit of peace*: In our sin-twisted world we all sometimes appear to others as opinionated, stubborn, and just plain silly, and sometimes we really are all three; and in every community, family, church, club, or whatever, it takes work to stay together in goodwill. It should not surprise us, then, to find that New Testament churches, while bubbling with excitement at the gospel that had brought them into being, were racked with internal relational problems. Paul has to beg them over and over to practice love, peace, mutual forbearance, and harmony as a discipline of union with each other in Christ. (See Rom. 12:9–10, 16; 15:5–6; 2 Cor. 13:11; Eph. 4:1–3; Phil. 1:27; 2:2; 4:2; 1 Thess. 5:13.) Human nature does not change, and affectionate harmony remains a fundamental demand of life together in Christ: a demand that can only be met through self-control and resolute effort.

Second, *the practicing of fellowship*: Christians who worship together can easily fall short here, not recognizing how we need each other's active help and support for full spiritual health. *Fellowship* (Greek, *koinonia*) is the New Testament word for helping each other by sharing. Fellowship means that I give you what God has given me, passing it on as my gift of care and help to you, and you respond in kind as your gift of care and help to me, so that the bond and benefit that we now have in common is more than either of us had when we started. This give-and-take is the fellowship that comes from the Holy Spirit, which, following Paul in 2 Corinthians 13:14, we pray that we may constantly enjoy, along with the grace that comes from the Lord Jesus and the love that comes from God the Father himself. By such fellowshipping we significantly pastor each other, and are significantly pastored, in the church all the time. Regular worshippers who see church life simply as a comfort zone where steady routine and ongoing bonhomie make them feel good week by week can wholly miss this quality of life together. In that case, despite their loyalty to the church as an institution, they have not yet started to express true Christian unity—unity in Christ with all Christ's people—at all. They are, sadly, a drag on the church's real life.

Third, *mutual help between churches*: Congregations that see each other as united together in Christ should be ready for mutual assistance, though how this plays out will depend on local needs. Because Jewish Christians in Jerusalem were impoverished, Paul took up a collection for them in the mainly Gentile churches that he founded, and he made a big issue of their giving from what they had as an expression of both unity in Christ and gratitude for Christ (see Acts 24:17; Rom. 15:25–28; 1 Cor. 16:1–4; 2 Corinthians 8–9). Such patterns of partnership and help express unity, advance the gospel, and glorify God. (This is what the Anglican diocesan system is meant to facilitate, though it does not always achieve success and credibility in its endeavors.)

Fourth, *an open Communion table*: Sharing the Supper is the one act of regular worship together that the Lord Jesus explicitly required of his disciples (1 Cor. 11:23–25). Visitors to a congregation who are in good standing in their home churches should be welcomed to express Christian unity with their hosts in this way, just as Paul and his party en route to Jerusalem were welcomed to the breaking of bread by the church at Troas (Acts 20:7–12). As is often and rightly said, it is the Lord's Table, not ours, and we should show hospitality there to all whose base congregations, with which we share unity in Christ, have judged us fit for Eucharistic fellowship. We can respect the jealousy for God's truth and glory that leads some to "fence the table" against those not of their own denominational stripe, but this obscures unity in Christ rather than expressing it. Modern Anglicanism takes the right line here, and so, with very few exceptions, do evangelicals as a body.

CHRISTIAN UNITY AND ANGLICAN UNITY

At the time of the Reformation, the establishing of the Thirty-Nine Articles alongside the ecumenical creeds (the Apostles', the Nicene-Constantinopolitan, and the Athanasian) as a domestic rule of faith, and the provision of a carefully and biblically Reformed Book of Common Prayer, were seen as securing for the Church of England unity in Christ with all the other churches of the magisterial Reformation, and this unity was acknowledged as a fact by all parties for the next three hundred years. Muddying the waters somewhat for the next hundred years (mid-nineteenth to mid-twentieth century) was the novel Anglo-Catholic insistence that unity in Christ is incomplete without an episcopate in the apostolic succession, such as Rome claims to have; but this idea, though loudly trumpeted, never became part of the Anglican standard of teaching. (Officially, Anglicanism stops short at valuing episcopacy as a God-honored pastoral institution for leadership and oversight, and as a visible link with the Christian past that it would be pointless and misleading to throw away.) The younger Anglican provinces, the fruit of devoted evangelical and Anglo-Catholic missionary work, have grown up and come of age within the mainstream of historically defined Anglican doctrine, and it is this doctrine that remains the constitutional standard for Anglicans everywhere right up to today. Here, then, is Anglicanism's formal frame of Christian unity.

But the past half century has seen the emergence—and in North America especially, both sides of the forty-ninth parallel, the dominance—of a type of theology, calling itself *liberal*, that does not acknowledge biblical authority, or the Trinity, or the incarnation, or the atonement; or the resurrection, reign, and coming return of Christ; or personal salvation in and through Christ; or the calling of the church to holiness and evangelism, in a way that squares with historic Reformed Anglican belief. It minimizes the uniqueness of the gospel and pursues assimilation of other world faiths of a pantheistic or panentheistic sort: Hinduism, Sikhism, and some forms of Buddhism, for starters. And it maintains, as one might expect, a scarcely veiled hostility to conservative versions of the Christian faith.

This revisionism, which was (and, it seems, still is) riding high in North American Anglican seminaries, effectively disrupted the solid-looking Christian unity of the Anglican Communion more than a generation ago. Now it expresses itself by, in general, baptizing the world into the church, as you might put it, and, in particular, reclassifying same-sex unions as no longer a breach of the order of creation and off-limits as such, but as a mode of holiness which the church ought to bless. For nonrevisionist Anglicans, this is a sanctifying of sin, which maims the gospel by eliminating one area of necessary repentance (see 1 Cor. 6:9–11), thus putting souls in danger. It is pastoral compassion, rather than homophobia, that has prompted the sense of shock at this and the firmness of opposition to it that has marked so many thoughtful people within global Anglicanism once they realized what was going on. Realignments began and are still in process.

What remains clear and certain in all this is that Christian unity starts with the authority of Scripture and the truth about Jesus Christ, as the Bible teaches it and as the Patristic creeds and Reformation confessions, echoing Scripture, define it; that the reimagining of God and the gospel by today's revisionists shatters that unity; and that only a reembracing of biblical doctrine as transcultural truth and of biblical behavior standards as abidingly authoritative will restore it. It is in these terms, therefore, that we must pray and work to rebuild Christian unity in our time.

> Lord, have mercy upon us.
> *Christ, have mercy upon us.*
> Lord, have mercy upon us.
> *Amen.*

QUESTIONS FOR STUDY AND DISCUSSION

1. In your opinion, are churchgoers sufficiently aware of the importance of Christian unity? If not, why not?
2. How would you relate Christian unity to Christian orthodoxy, church union, and Christian fellowship?
3. How can you promote Christian unity in your own congregation?
4. How can you further Christian unity among the churches with which your congregation is most closely linked?
5. Do you agreed that blessing same-sex unions is a breach of Christian unity? If so, how would you answer those who deny this? If not, how would you answer those who regard the breach as real?
6. What do you think are the most important elements in one's personal practice of Christian unity?

4

TAKING REPENTANCE
SERIOUSLY

As I write this, three declarations are jumping up and down in my mind. The first is the call of my title, to take repentance seriously. The second, dating from half a millennium ago, is the first of Luther's Ninety-Five Theses (1517), which sparked the European Reformation: "When our Lord and Master Jesus Christ said, 'Repent,' he meant the whole life of a believer to be a practice of repentance." The third is a book title from the not-so-distant past: *The Church Must First Repent*.

Between them, these three declarations express most of what I want to say now.

REPENTANCE IS BASIC

But how am I to say it? Where should I start? The problem is that teaching, talk, and thought about repentance have virtually vanished, not just from our post-Christian secular world, but from the lives of church people too. The words *repent* and *repentance*, which we hear often enough in church services, carry no clear meaning to us; in fact, they signify something to which most of us are strangers. Rarely if ever do we hear sermons about repentance (check your own memory for that); rarely if ever do we talk to each other about repentance; like sex in the Victorian era and death in the twentieth century, it has become a Great Unmentionable. The nearest many of us get to it is the sour old proverb that, perhaps I may say, we half know, "Marry in haste, repent at leisure," where "repent" means "wish we hadn't done it" (only a skewed fraction of the word's Christian mean-ing, by the way)—and beyond this our thinking about repentance does not go.

Which is an amazing thing, when we weigh the following facts:

1. THE CALL TO REPENT WAS THE BEGINNING OF THE PREACHING OF THE BIBLICAL GOSPEL

John the Baptist's message from the start, we are told, was, "Repent, for the kingdom of heaven is at hand" (Matt. 3:2). After John's imprisonment Jesus "began to preach, saying, 'Repent, for the king-dom of heaven is at hand'" (Matt. 4:17). When Jesus sent the Twelve on their first mission, they "proclaimed that people should repent" (Mark 6:12). When on resurrection day evening Jesus appeared to the disciples, "he opened their minds to understand the Scriptures, and said to them, 'Thus it is written, that the Christ should suffer and on the third day rise from the dead, and that repentance and forgiveness of sins should be proclaimed in his name to all nations'" (Luke 24:45–47; not, note, forgiveness without repentance!). When on Pentecost morning Peter's Spirit-empowered sermon so stirred the crowd that they interrupted him, asking what they needed to do, his first word in reply was, "Repent" (Acts 2:38). Paul described his extended ministry at Ephesus as one of "testifying both to Jews and to Greeks of repentance toward God and of faith in our Lord Jesus Christ" (Acts 20:21; again, not faith without repentance!). And he told King Agrippa that he had simply been proclaiming to one and all "that they should repent and turn to God, performing deeds in keep-ing with their repentance" (Acts 26:20). So in Athens, the intellectual capital of the ancient world, Paul had told the Areopagus, the top gathering of Athens's intellectual elite, that "God . . . now . . . com-mands all people everywhere to repent" (Acts 17:30). Repentance was thus primary in the preaching of John, of Jesus, of Peter, and of Paul, and Peter's last words on paper include the description of Jesus as "not wishing that any should perish, but that all should reach repentance" (2 Pet. 3:9). The centrality of repentance in the gospel and purpose of Jesus Christ our Lord is a fact we must face.

2. THE CALL TO REPENT WAS THE BEGINNING OF THE SIXTEENTH-CENTURY REFORMATION

Constantly and correctly we are told that the heart of Reformation theology, the theology that determined the shape of the Anglican Book of Common Prayer, was its reconceiving of faith. Hereby faith came to mean, not just believing the creed, but on that basis trusting oneself to God's promises of pardon and peace through Jesus Christ the crucified and risen Lord, who died on the cross for our sins. This trust is an embrace of Christ himself, whereby as we cling to him he receives us, and faith becomes the mainspring of a new life of obedient discipleship. Without this trust, said the Reformers, there is no faith; credence without commitment does not constitute faith. In England, in the days of Henry VIII and Edward VI, this Reformed theology was actually called the doctrine of faith rather than of justification, which is what it was called in Lutheran territory.

Now my present point is that Reformation theology can just as validly be described as a reconceiving of repentance. Previously, repentance had been taken to mean confessing your sins to a priest with suitable sorrow, receiving absolution from him, and performing whatever "penance" (corrective discipline) he might impose. In Reformation thought, however, faith and repentance were brought together, back-to-back as it were, like the two sides of a single coin, and repentance became the comprehensive, habitual turning away from sin to serve Christ in righteousness that the gospel demands and faith energizes. Luther's nugget assertion of this has already been quoted, and here is a statement made in 1549 by Archbishop Thomas Cranmer, chief architect of the Book of Common Prayer, that amplifies the same idea: "Repentance for sins according to the gospel [*Evangelice*] is a saving [*salutaris*, health-giving] grief about one's sins because of their offence to God, with hope of obtaining pardon through Christ and a purpose of amending one's life with Christ's help" (my translation of Cranmer's Latin in Ashley Null, *Thomas Cranmer's Doctrine of Repentance* [Oxford: Oxford University Press, 2000], 237, n. 100). Without serious effort to change one's ways, said the Reformers, repentance is not real; mere bewailing and confessing and breast-beating with remorse and regret still fall short of it. So the centrality of repentance in our Reformational understanding of Christianity is another fact we must face.

3. THE CALL TO REPENT IS THE BEGINNING OF ANGLICAN LITURGICAL WORSHIP

"Anglican liturgical worship" is a phrase covering the many versions of Cranmer's Book of Common Prayer (first form 1549, second form 1552) and England's classic 1662 revision of it. Canada's Book of Common Prayer, published in 1962, is in fact 1662 with minor omissions, additions, and adjustments. All Prayer Book services aim at two things together: the honor and glory of God and the sanctification of the worshippers, that is, their formation in a holy life on the basis of the forgiveness of their sins through faith in Christ and the embracing of repentance as their path of life for the future. Thus, Morning and Evening Prayer, the daily Bible services, begin with a confession of sin that ends with the words: "Restore thou them that are *penitent* [i.e., repentant]; According to thy promises declared unto mankind in Christ Jesus our Lord. And grant, O most merciful Father, for his sake, That we may hereafter live a godly, righteous, and sober life, To the glory of thy holy Name" (emphasis added, here and below). To this the absolution that follows responds by declaring that we ask God "to grant us true *repentance* and his Holy Spirit . . . that the rest of our life hereafter may be pure and holy; so that at the last we may come to his eternal joy; through Jesus Christ our Lord."

In the two-part Holy Communion service, the Ante-Communion (to give it its old name) starts with prayer for the cleansing of our hearts "that we may perfectly love thee," and for the law of God to be written on our hearts; and the Communion proper begins with an invitation to those "who do truly and earnestly *repent* you of your sins," leading into a confession of sin that centers upon the following: "We do earnestly *repent*, And are heartily sorry for these our misdoings . . . . Forgive us all that is past; And grant that we may ever hereafter Serve and please thee in newness of life, To the honor and glory of thy Name."

And the prayer of absolution that follows invokes God as "our heavenly Father, who of his great mercy hath promised forgiveness of sins to all them that with hearty *repentance* and true faith turn unto him." Then in the Litany, the first part of Cranmer's liturgy to be composed, we ask God to "give us true *repentance*; to forgive us all our sins, negligences and ignorances; and to endue us with the grace of thy Holy Spirit, to amend our lives according to thy holy Word."

Also, the Book of Common Prayer contains "A Penitential Service for Use on Ash Wednesday and at other times," in which we pray that "we, truly *repenting* of our sins, may obtain of thee perfect pardon and release." This indeed is something of a drumbeat emphasis throughout Anglicanism's authorized liturgy.

In the Canadian *Book of Alternative Services* the emphasis on repentance as basic to devotion is very much weakened, which is surely something to regret, but it is there still, as the postbaptismal Reconciliation of a Penitent ([Toronto, Canada: Anglican Book Centre, 1985], 166–72), and the Eucharistic Penitential Order (pp. 216–17), to look no further, show us.

What emerges from what we have seen thus far, however, is that a generation of churchgoers like ourselves, who know so little about repenting, are spiritually superficial by historic Anglican standards and devotionally very much out of sorts. Prayer Book Christianity is Bible Christianity, and Bible Christianity is founded on repentance, just as it is built on faith, and we are today falling badly short. So we must think our way through this subject from square one. That means, we must start with God, the Holy Lord, from whom we learn the nature of sin.

THE HUMAN CONDITION

The passages cited from the New Testament told us that repentance is *toward God*, and the Book of Common Prayer tells us that what we must repent of is the sins for which we seek forgiveness—our *misdoings*, that is, both by commission and by omission. The Bible's big story, which binds all its contents together—what nowadays is called its metanarrative—tells us to understand these misdoings in the following terms: God has made (formed) humans in his own image, meaning us to behave toward him and each other in a way that reflects his own character of love and justice, truthfulness and trustworthiness, creativity and joy in work. But a corrupting force in our moral and spiritual system, with a corrupt demonic intelligence behind it, has unmade (deformed) us all, so that now we are alienated from God and have become a grotesque and, alas, vicious travesty of what we were meant to be. The Bible's name for the deforming force, both in itself and in its various modes of expression, is sin. Through Christ the Redeemer we can be remade—restored, that is, to God's fellowship here and now, and started on the road of being reconformed to God's image by learning to live Christlike lives. Repentance, in the broadest sense, signifies that change of mind, purpose, attitude, and behavior whereby we embrace God's agenda of mercy toward us and turn back from the old life of fighting God by playing God to live the new life of humbly and thankfully serving him. Repentance is thus a whole-person business in which a pattern of self-centered self-service is replaced by a God-centered habit of seeking others' welfare, and pride and willfulness give way to prayer and worship.

But now, within this new frame of life, each act of repenting is specific. I discern in myself a particular fault, shortcoming, type of misbehavior, bad habit, or whatever. I ask forgiveness for it, through

Christ's atonement, telling God that I am asking also for help to break the pattern: to be different henceforth and not lapse again, and meantime to see and do all I can do to make amends for the damage, both relational and material, that my past lapses actually caused. This is the reality of repenting that we are concerned to explore, the repenting to which the Bible and the Prayer Book summon us in the name of the Lord Jesus himself.

To make the reality of repenting clearer, more must be said about sin. Be warned: some of what the next few paragraphs will affirm may sound to you shocking and incredible. That is because, as a result of sin's deceitfulness (more of that in a moment), we know so little about ourselves. In our therapeutically oriented Western culture, where Christian perspectives are largely lost, we settle for comparing ourselves with each other, inevitably from the outside only and in merely behavioral terms. We think of ourselves as basically good and certainly better than some people we know, and we really have no idea how we appear to a holy God who searches hearts and knows us literally inside out. As scanners in hospitals put our physical insides on display for physicians to see, so the eyes of the Creator scan our hearts and show up the thoughts, motives, dreams, drives, cravings, fantasies, hates, hostilities, and meannesses that actually make us tick, including those of which we are only half-aware and indeed those of which we are not aware at all till someone brings them to our notice. The first time I saw my physical heart on a screen, thumping away, as they scanned me, it was a jolt, and every time one gets a glimpse of one's personal heart (inner spirit) as God sees it, churning out perversities of all kinds, that will jolt one too. God's view of us is not complimentary, and our pride makes it difficult at first for us to accept what he tells us about ourselves. But if we are humble and honest, we shall end up accepting it, for we shall find ourselves convinced that the cap fits, and God's diagnosis of us is true.

The wide range of words in Hebrew and Greek that our Bibles

translate as "sin" express the ideas of failing either to hit a target or to reach a standard or to obey authority or to be clean in company. And the standard unreached, the target missed, the path abandoned, the law transgressed, the authority defied, and the purity violated are God's. God's character and will are the true measure of sin.

The way of sin is to live, not for God, but for yourself; to love and serve and please yourself without regard for your Maker; to try to be independent of him, to hold him at arm's length, to keep the reins of your own life firmly in your own hands; yet at the same time to try to manipulate him as a means to your own ends and to use him as a safety net when you are in trouble. Sin is truly the Devil's image in us, for self-exalting, God-defying pride was his before ever it was ours (1 Tim. 3:6). Sin is deviation from the God who wants our fellowship and worship, and sin embraces self-absorption in place of God-centeredness. Augustine spoke of *homo incurvatus in se*, the human self bent in upon oneself. The historic name for our inborn antipathy to God and his law is *original* sin (*peccatum originale*, another phrase coined by Augustine). The name, though not found in Scripture, is entirely appropriate, whether we take it as signifying that this disposition comes to us from the first human or simply that it is in us from the moment of our origin and that in any case all our acts of sin stem from it. The sinful condition of human-kind, according to the Bible, is absolutely universal. "There is no one who does not sin" (1 Kings 8:46). "All, both Jews and Greeks, are under sin . . . : None is righteous . . . . No one does good . . . . All have sinned and fall short of the glory of God" (Rom. 3:9–12, 23). All human beings are guilty and unclean in God's sight.

This spirit of sin within us, which disrupts the relationship between us and our Creator, disrupts human society also. From self-aggrandizing nonlove of God springs self-aggrandizing nonlove of neighbor. Irreligion breeds inhumanity. Sin spreads and society suffers. Think about Paul's three sad catalogs of characteristic forms that this disruption takes (Rom. 1:26–31; Gal. 5:19–21; and 2 Tim.

3:2–4), and also about Jesus's list of defiling things that come out of the human heart (Mark 7:20–23). Every item in those lists can be matched in the Western world today.

To sum up: sin, as a label for our natural state before God, signifies rebellion, defilement, condemnation, and slavery. *Rebellion* means that all of us resent, defy, evade, belittle, ignore, and disobey God, one way or another, every day of our lives. *Defilement* means that all of us are unclean—dirty, to say it straight out—in God's sight; we are offensive and unacceptable to him, and unfit for his fellowship. *Condemnation* means that in the presence of God our Judge we are all guilty rebels who can now only await the moment when God makes us feel his displeasure. *Slavery*—you could call it bondage, or addiction—means that we are all naturally under sin's power; we do not have it in us to love God and our neighbor wholeheartedly and without qualification, the way we should. And only through a faith-and-repentance relationship with the Lord Jesus, a relationship that brings forgiveness and renews our hearts, can this slavery ever be ended.

Such, then, is the frame of insight into the human condition within which repentance, both personal and corporate, is to be understood. Repentance, we now see, will always be more than a moment of regret and remorse, plus a word of apology; it will always center upon turning from and leaving behind what was wrong, and asking God in fullest sincerity to keep us from ever falling back into this wrongness again. The world of spiritual reality into which our thinking has led us, we now see, is the world of sin and grace: of the sin that will ruin us, keeping us from knowing the joy of God's love forever unless Christ saves us, and of the grace that will rescue us from sin's guilt and power through Christ's death, resurrection, and gift of the Holy Spirit. I now cast anchor explicitly in this biblical world of sin and grace, toward which I have been navigating from the start; and I give notice that I shall remain in it for the rest of this study.

PERSONAL REPENTANCE: THE HABIT AND THE FIGHT

"Sow an action, reap a habit; sow a habit, reap a character; sow a character, reap a destiny." The words of the proverb apply directly. Repentance is an action that must become a habit and a mark of character in each Christian's life, as we shall now see.

Neither the Bible nor the Book of Common Prayer gives us a formal definition of personal repentance. But here is a time-honored one, taken from the Shorter Catechism of the mid-seventeenth-century Westminster Assembly, a body 90 percent of whose members were Anglican clergymen: "Repentance unto life is a saving grace, whereby a sinner, out of a true sense of his sin, and apprehension of the mercy of God in Christ, doth, with grief and hatred of his sin, turn from it unto God, with full purpose of, and endeavour after, new obedience." This definition, given in answer to question 87, pulls together all we have said so far. It applies to each repetition of repentance throughout the Christian's life, for every act of repenting is "unto life" in the sense that penitents know they must surrender their sins in order to be saved. And the statement provides a launch-pad for what has to be said now.

Repentance, like sin, begins as a desire of the heart. "*Hearty* [that is, heartfelt] repentance and *true* faith" are called for, according to the Book of Common Prayer, when we turn in humility to God. The regenerate heart is a battlefield, where the Spirit-wrought desire to please God and the residual twisted desire to please oneself are constantly slugging it out. Sin within deceives us, desensitizing us about the evil of what we are doing till after we have done it. (See the pattern in the story of the fall, Genesis 3, and note Rom. 7:11; Heb. 3:13.) Paul speaks of the need to renounce "deceitful desires" (Eph. 4:22). Sin will paralyze thought, so mesmerizing us by the dazzling prospects it offers that reason and conscience cannot get a word in edgewise. (Later we shall say, "I didn't *think*—I acted in a moment of *thoughtlessness*"—and how right we shall be.) Sins of exploiting people, manipulating systems, ducking responsibilities, withholding goodwill, and working out resentments to gain revenge regularly reflect a mind switched off, a state of affairs to which alcohol, drugs, and exhaustion can contribute alarmingly.

Habitual yielding to sin's alluring blandishments will blind and harden us. (For this biblical picture, see again Heb. 3:13, with Eph. 4:18–19; 1 Tim. 4:2.) This is the process whereby one's conscience ceases to function with regard to particular things one is up to, or the attitudes of pride, godlessness, lovelessness, brutality, hatred, contempt, dishonesty, untruthfulness, or whatever that one is indulging. The habit of going against conscience soon kills conscience, so that spiritual blindness and hardening become ever-deeper realities in one's life.

Countermeasures must take the form of thought, prayer, meditating on the Scriptures, keeping close and becoming transparent to fellow-believers, and making a point of repenting—formally, frankly, and fully, in an explicit transaction with God—the moment we realize that we have in any way gone wrong. Hereby we set up defenses against sin's further attacks, as the battle goes on.

The habit of regular self-examination—that is, of periodically opening ourselves to God so as to learn from him through the Bible what our track record looks like to his all-seeing eyes—will help to keep us realistic at this point. The psalmist's prayer—"Search me, O God, and know my heart! / Try me and know my thoughts! / And see if there be any grievous way in me, / and lead me in the way everlasting!" (Ps. 139:23–24)—is a model for us all. Sin is multiform and chameleon-like in the way it presents itself as good, but disordered and, to use the church's old word, inordinate desire is always at its root, and a clearheaded taxonomy of desires will be helpful whenever we give ourselves this periodic once-over. Thus, desire for sex, for food and drink, and for ease and comfort are sample desires of the body that can lead us astray. Desire for profit, for possessions and wealth, for mastery and control in some specific area, for reputation and respect, and for the power of the top position, whether as leader or as the critic who undermines and cuts down the leader, are sample desires of the mind that trip us up. Each of us will need to compile our own list of what our own self-knowledge, such as it is, tells us to watch out for in the way of personal weaknesses. By thus making self-examination a habit and reinstating it as one of the disciplines of the Christian life, we are likely to do better in our inner war with sin than we shall if we fail to do this. So here is wisdom for our pilgrimage.

I turn now to the implications for our corporate life of the things I have been saying.

THE STATE OF THE CHURCH

The first question here must be, on what part of the worldwide church of Christ are we to focus our attention? The church on earth at this time is a very large and varied body, with a number of cultural and convictional differences built into its makeup. Speaking roughly, of its over two billion members, a billion and a quarter are Roman Catholics, a quarter of a billion are Eastern Orthodox, and half a billion are Protestants of one sort or another, mostly conservative evangelicals with more or less of a Pentecostal style. Something like a sixth of them are Anglicans. In the "Old West" of Britain, Canada, the United States, Australasia, and South Africa, where English is the common language and cultural links with England are, or have been, strongest, approximately half of those who call themselves Anglicans do not regularly attend church, appearing only for special occasions. Thus, about four million "Old Westerners" join in public worship on an average Sunday, as compared with some forty million worshipping in younger Anglican churches in Africa, Asia, and South America. Until recently the "Old West" gave theological, pastoral, and devotional leadership to the Anglican Communion as a whole, though this is changing.

The essays contained in this book mostly come from, and

therefore were at first largely addressed to, the Anglican Church of Canada, a body less than two-thirds of a million strong and only one-quarter the size of the Episcopal Church, its counterpart in the United States. It is a province of the Anglican Communion in its own right and is noticeably distinct in spirit, style, and sociological contour from its bigger brother south of the border, just as indeed Canada itself is. The ACC will be the specific center of attention in what follows; however, writer and publisher both believe that what is being said has a relevance far beyond the ACC's borders.

A century ago, the ACC was more like the then Church of England, intellectually, pastorally, and institutionally, than is the case today. On its two wings, as in England, were evangelicals (low church) and Anglo-Catholics (high church), each viewing the other as its polar opposite, spiritually stunted through the limitations of its theology, and each thinking of itself as having a better right to lead the church than any other group. Evangelicals criticized Anglo-Catholics for not understanding personal conversion and life in the Holy Spirit's power, and Anglo-Catholics criticized evangelicals for not understanding the church, the sacraments, and the disciplines of true devotion. Both had their theological colleges, societies, and what may fairly be called power bases. Each was precise in formulating its own account of the redemption and regeneration, through the grace of Jesus Christ our Lord, of human creatures ruined by sin, and each was confident of the accuracy and adequacy of its own biblical interpretation and theological heritage. Then, in the center, forming the majority at both membership and leadership level, were the "broad" churchmen, loyal to the Anglican tradition and institution but seeing both parties on the wings as narrow, rigid extremists (as, no doubt, some were), and laying more emphasis on the church's social tasks and less on the individual's communion with Christ than either of the other groups did.

Two generations ago, so it seems, serious attempts began to be made to mute both wings and extend the solidarity of the center, in the belief that this was what the ACC needed. The result was that, with little debate happening to keep minds sharp, Anglican Christianity became fuzzy at the edges. Specifically, it became unsure about biblical authority in light of biblical criticism, imprecise regarding the doctrines of the creeds, loose regarding the life of faith in Christ and the discipline of personal repentance, and neglectful of Anglicanism's earlier educational priority of clergy teaching and layfolk learning aspects of Christian truth throughout their life. Living in the shadow of both stiffly authoritarian Roman Catholicism and the robust liberalism of the United Church, the ACC became increasingly genial, friendly, and relaxed in style, but increasingly less attentive to catechetical instruction, evangelistic outreach, spiritual formation, and serious theology. After half a century of this, a great deal of lost ground now needs to be made up.

During this past century, Canada has ceased to identify itself as a Christian country, calling itself multicultural and multireligious instead, and national life has drifted far from its Christian moorings. Both evangelicals and Anglo-Catholics have recovered some strength and now see each other as, in most respects, brothers and allies. Meantime, a virulent version of liberal theology has emerged, reducing the historical facts of faith to symbols signifying personal religious intuitions, embracing cultural driftings as new revelations of God's mind and will, and seeking on this basis to create a theosophical theology that assimilates all religions to each other. The inevitable clash between the conservationist and revisionist agendas came about on gay sexual ethics: whether the church should approve and bless same-sex partnerships, even viewing them as marriages, in line with present Canadian public law, or not. Over this issue, and the conception of the gospel that goes with each view, the entire Anglican Communion, along with the ACC itself, is now split, and it will have to be reshaped. Truly we live, as the Chinese euphemism puts it, in interesting times.

CORPORATE REPENTANCE: THE VISION

The books of the prophets constitute about a quarter of the Old Testament and a fifth of the Bible as a whole. In most printings, while the Epistles fill about a hundred pages and the Gospels 120, the fifteen prophetic books, spanning four centuries and ranging from Isaiah's sixty-six-chapter colossus to tiny one-chapter Obadiah, occupy some 250. This amount of space itself tells us that these books are important. When we read them, we find that the prophets are much more moralists than futurologists, and what they speak constantly about is corporate repentance, made necessary by communal sin. God's recurring message to Israel through them, in consolidated form, boils down to this:

- *I am your covenant God.* I have chosen you, redeemed you from slavery, given you this land, and promised you protection and prosperity in it. Never forget my mercy in this.
- *I require you to keep my law always, for I am your holy Lord and Judge.* ("Holy" in the Bible is an umbrella word signifying all that makes God awesome and sometimes fearsome to us, notably his boundless power, absolute purity, and impeccable justice. Human holiness is faithful law keeping in a frame of fellowship with God.)
- *I have discerned in you disbelief of my words and disobedience to them, and I promise you disaster as my punitive, purging judgment for that; after which I guarantee to restore a repentant remnant under a ruler who will prove himself to be David redivivus. If you hope for a share in the good things to come, return to me now!* ("Turn" and "return" are the Old Testament words that express the meaning of "repent" in the New Testament.)

Chapters 1–3 of the New Testament book called Revelation echo all this in a Christian context. Here our Lord Jesus Christ, the church's glorified Head, sends through John business letters to seven Asia Minor congregations. The letters assess their achievements, note their failings, and tell five of them to repent of particular short-comings or be pulverized in judgment; after which, all are encouraged by a promise of eternal bliss with the Lord himself for all who "conquer"—that is, who say a firm *no* to sin and error, who uphold gospel truth as Christ and his apostles gave it, and who practice faithful obedience to it, despite all persuasions and pressures to do something else instead.

Again and again, as we read the Bible, we have to ask ourselves, If that is what our unchanging God said to those people/that person then, what should we conclude that he has to say to us now? When we put this question to Revelation 1–3, where does it take us? In the present state of the ACC, as in much of the church worldwide, it seems an inescapable inference that our Lord's call to all of us at this moment, loud and clear, is "Repent!" In light of what we have surveyed in these pages, we can flesh that out a little. It is as if our Lord should say to our Anglican Church, and to all of us who are part of it—and here you could put the name of your own church—which is of course his church really:

"Return to *me*, the One who is the same yesterday, today, and forever. From the Gospels and from letters like Colossians and Ephesians and Hebrews renew your vision of who and what I am, and from your starting point in Revelation 1–3 renew your sense of, and your sensitivity to, the things I have to tell you. You seem to be out of range of my voice; come closer, listen harder, and get back under my supremacy and authority. Learn from me the destructive force of all the proud foolishness that has seeped into the church. Follow me as I lead you away from it.

"Return to *truth*, that is to my teaching and the Bible's teaching. Here is truth for everyone, truth through which reality is found and I myself become known. The idea that there is no universal truth, but that when it comes to life strategies it is everyone for himself intellectually, is a postmodern fantasy, flattering perhaps but totally confusing and totally wrong. The key truths of the gospel, that I was man in Palestine and was crucified to save sinners, have always given offense and always will, but these are the life truths of fact that everyone needs to know. So begin your repenting with your mind, practice intellectual repentance for uncritically accepting fashionable intellectual folly, confess the mental mistakes that you picked up from the pagan world around you and forsake them; and follow me into renewed faithfulness to the true truth of God.

"Finally, return to *holiness*. Holiness means consecration, seeking always to do right and avoid sinning. So steel yourself against slothfulness, carelessness, apathy, drifting, halfheartedness, double-mindedness, and spineless conformity to the world. Turn your back on the world's slack standards—all forms, for instance, of irresponsible sexual self-indulgence and promiscuity. With that, turn your eyes away from all forms of pornography and secret sexual stimulation, which are the stepping-stones into that indulgence. And turn your heart away from all forms of dishonesty and evading proper responsibility in all personal relationships and all business transactions, and from all forms of behavior that cheapen life itself. Say good-bye to your complacency about your present condition. Humbly practice self-examination, with willingness to have the Spirit through the Word and Christians in the fellowship show you where you are off track and falling short. Learn from my example to love sinners by trying to wean them away from their sinning, which I hate, and which you must learn to hate too. Watch me in action in the Gospels, and seek always to advance in knowing, loving, adoring, and imitating me, so as to please my Father in all that you do. Let go of distractions that clutter your life; pass up petty things, and think and pray big, even though circumstances may compel you to act small. Express your unity with all believing people, and do all the good you can to all those around you. Be zealous to extend my kingdom, serving the saints, practicing Samaritanship with strangers, and laboring to spread the gospel everywhere. Stay put with me in my risen life, share your daily tasks with me, look to me for help at each step, and I will walk with you all the way. Follow me, then, with a well-schooled conscience that you keep clean, and more and more of the power and peace that I give will be shown forth in you."

So now, are we going to take repentance seriously? What might we expect for ourselves and our church if we do, and what if we don't? Over to you.

QUESTIONS FOR STUDY AND DISCUSSION

1. What is your definition of repentance?
2. How do you understand the holiness of God?
3. Do you think the stress on repentance in Prayer Book worship is excessive?
4. Was G. K. Chesterton right when he affirmed that original sin is the one Christian doctrine that can be proved and established anywhere by simple, direct inspection?
5. What problems might be raised concerning the biblical view of sin? How would you deal with them?
6. If you believe that the Anglican Church of Canada—or your own affiliation, if another—needs to repent, what can you do about it?

TAKING THE CHURCH
SERIOUSLY

> Almighty God, we beseech thee graciously to behold this thy family, for which our Lord Jesus Christ was contented to be betrayed, and given up into the hands of wicked men, and to suffer death upon the cross; who now liveth and reigneth with thee and the Holy Spirit, ever one God, world without end. Amen.
>
> (First Good Friday collect, Book of
> Common Prayer, 1962, Canada)

GRACE AND THE CHURCH

The first step in taking the church seriously must be to recognize that most often when the word *church* enters our mind or exits our mouth, this is precisely not what we are doing.

When we use the word as a label for a building (e.g., St. John's Church) or a denomination (e.g., the Anglican Church), or for a do-gooding group of religious people among whom we find stability and support when we are frazzled (i.e., our own congregation), or when we say on Sunday morning that we are going to church and at lunch that we have been to church, we are as yet quite a distance from the full Christian meaning that the term carries in the New Testament. That, however, is what we are now to seek; and to find it, we cannot do better than turn to Paul's letter to the Ephesians, where from one standpoint the church is the highlighted theme.

They say that the best way to learn something is to teach it, and that is my story here. Through an odd set of circumstances, before ever I started studying theology academically, I was set to teach a class of ordinands to translate and exegete the Greek text of

Ephesians in preparation for an exam that they had to pass before being ordained. They all passed, I am glad to say, and through this experience I became the Ephesians man to my fingertips that I am today.

Ephesians is a tremendously powerful piece of writing, as you can prove for yourself by thoughtfully reading it through ten times without stopping. (Is that a challenge? Yes.) The twin themes that bind its two halves together—the doctrine, praise, and prayer half in chapters 1–3 and the practical, faithfulness, and obedience half in chapters 4–6—are the *grace* of God and the *church* of God, the former theme framing and undergirding the latter, and the latter theme putting the former on large-scale display. We shall now follow Paul as he zeroes in on grace; that is the most direct way to an understanding of the church, as we shall see.

What is *grace*? The word (*charis* in Greek) is a Christian technical term. Its pre-Christian meaning was gracefulness, elegance, and charm, and it was not a word of importance. But in Paul's letters in particular, as evidently also in the regular vocabulary of the Christians to whom he wrote (otherwise they would not have understood him), *charis* has become the standard label for the attitude and action of *God in love saving sinners*. That was something that the world knew nothing of until Christianity arrived on the scene. So, because it now carried a new meaning, *charis* became in effect a new word.

To spell this out, as Paul does in Ephesians:

God sees the human race living, so to speak, with their backs to him, offending him right, left, and center by ignoring his instruction and practicing self-service according to their own fancy. Deep-rooted egocentricity, which is the essence of original sin, is an infection that no one escapes. And since we do not have it in us to respond positively to any divine word, whether law or gospel, and are in fact totally in the grip of the Devil, God counts us as dead, spiritually speaking, here and now (Eph. 2:1, 5).

But some of us, like Paul himself and those to whom he was writing, both Jews and non-Jews, are now alive to God! That is through God's grace, whereby in love he chose us to be his eternal companions, his sons, and his heirs; sent his divine Son into the world to die for our sins, so securing for us our new status of eternal reconciliation, forgiveness, and acceptance; brought us to life—personal spiritual responsiveness, that is—by uniting us to the Son in his resurrection life; and bonded us with each other in and through Christ as well (see Ephesians 1–2).

This is the inner reality of becoming a Christian. We are led to acknowledge the love of God the Father, the Son, and the Spirit; to realize the reality and presence with us of the Son, Jesus Christ, in the power of his atoning death and risen life; to trust him and his sacrifice for the cancelling of our guilt; to embrace him in penitent submission to be our Lord and Master from now on; and to love and serve our fellow-believers as our brothers and sisters in Christ.

For when we become Christians, we are not alone and must never think of ourselves as being alone. We are saved individually, one by one, but not for a life of solitary and still self-centered individualism. None of us is the only pebble on God's beach! On the contrary, we have been brought into a new solidarity: that of being, first, adopted children in the Father's family and, then, linked units in God's new creation through union with the risen Christ by the Holy Spirit. This new creation is the reality that is called the *church*.

GOD'S PLAN FOR THE CHURCH

Observe now how Paul presents the church in Ephesians. He begins to shine the light on it after declaring that God in grace—"because of the great love with which he loved us" (Eph. 2:4)—has given us spiritual life here and now, and set before us a glowing future destiny, by sovereignly uniting us to the risen Lord. "For by grace," he writes, "you have been saved through faith. . . . It is the gift of God . . . . For *we are his workmanship*, created in Christ Jesus for good works" (2:8–10). "Workmanship" (sometimes over-translated as "masterpiece," which signifies both more and less than Paul is expressing) is a word that carries two thoughts. The first is of creation in the sense of *construction*, as a poem, a painting, or a piece of music is a creative artist's construction. The second is of *conjunction*, solidarity resulting from the togetherness of people permanently involved with each other. "Workmanship" is a singular noun; it announces that what God has done for us individually has welded us into a single entity by virtue of the uniting link that each of us now has with Jesus Christ.

Three basic images, or analogies, each illustrating some ongoing aspect of the single entity created by the divine workmanship, now follow. These are the *building*, the *body*, and the *bride*. Each needs to be looked at separately to focus its distinct meaning.

The building. On the foundation of the apostles and prophets, with the Lord Jesus as the cornerstone, Gentile and Jewish believers are being built together, as so many building blocks or shaped stones laid side by side, to become "a holy temple in the Lord . . . *a dwelling place for God* by the Spirit" (2:20–22). As in Old Testament times the temple was where God made people most vividly aware of his self-revealed reality and teaching, and where they in turn knew themselves closest to him (see the Psalms), so it is and will ever be in the church. That is a fact that all Christians should face, and celebrate joyfully from the heart.

The body. As in the human body the head—meaning, the mind sustained by the brain inside the skull—animates, controls, directs, and integrates the action of the whole organism in its various parts, so the church, which is one body under Christ its Head, grows and upbuilds itself in faith and love through the harmonious operation of each particular body part. That is to say, as each believer seeks to attain total Christlikeness, and as the Holy Spirit of Christ prompts each to cooperative work and service out of love to God, to neighbors, and to the body of Christ as such, the church moves forward into "the unity of the faith and of the knowledge of the Son of God . . . to the measure of the stature of *the fullness of Christ*" (4:1–16, esp. 13). The vision is of divinely managed coordination of all who compose the body, of diversity of ministry within the unity of the body, and of developing discernment of the truth and wisdom of God by the body corporately. That is a goal that all Christians should embrace.

The bride. As the bride is prepared by willing helpers for her wedding day, so Christ himself, the church's Bridegroom, works to prepare the church, the object of his love, for the glory that he has in view for her—"that he might present the church to himself *in splendor*, without spot or wrinkle or any such thing, that she might *be holy and without blemish*" (5:25–27). Ongoing sanctification for all Christians, separately and together, through a vast variety of events, circumstances, and conflicts, is accordingly the church's present experience, while the approaching corporate consummation of fellowship with Jesus is the church's abiding hope, and the assurance of Jesus's unfailing love remains its constant support. That is an outlook, and an upward and forward look, that all Christians should cherish and keep intact.

This is the church that, according to the Nicene Creed, every Christian should believe in: that is, should recognize and confess as real, according to the Word of God. The creed uses four adjectives to describe it: *one, holy, catholic,* and *apostolic.*

One declares that the church is a single global community in, through, and under Jesus Christ its Lord; a community in which social, racial, creedal, and cultural differences between human individuals and groups are transcended, just as Paul says in Galatians 3:26–28.

Holy points to the church's consecration and commitment to the worship, obedience, and service of God, which is the central dimension of the active image of Christ, the Son of God, in all his disciples.

Catholic means, not Roman Catholic, but simply worldwide.

The word is there as a reminder that the church is in the world for the world, with a mission to the world; and thus the word stands as a roadblock against all forms of sectarianism and social or racial exclusiveness, or anything less than a global outlook. Also, increasingly in recent years "catholic" has been understood qualitatively, to signify holding to the fullness of the faith, as well as to the fullness of the mission; and this is as it should be.

Apostolic asserts authenticity of belief and purpose. On the one hand, it announces that the church holds to the doctrine taught by the apostles, and that bodies based on different beliefs (e.g., the unitarian churches, or the Mormon community, which styles itself the Church of Jesus Christ of Latter-day Saints) are no part of Christ's church, despite the fact that they claim the name. On the other hand, it declares that the church's abiding goal is to disciple all the nations according to the Great Commission that the risen Lord gave the apostles (Matt. 28:19–20).

Such is the church as God sees and knows it, and as it is set forth in the New Testament for us to see and know in this way too. It is the centerpiece of God's plan to display his mind-boggling wisdom and goodness to all the angelic powers (see Eph. 3:8–11), and it ought to be the central focus of our own thoughts as we seek to fulfill our vocation of glorifying God (that is, honoring, praising, and thanking him for his praiseworthiness) when we contemplate the blessings of our creation, preservation, and salvation. It needs to be said that Christians who do not recognize that the Christ-centeredness of their calling requires of them church-centeredness as a habit of mind are at that point really substandard.

THE CHURCH AND THE CHURCHES

What has been said has surely made us aware that, whereas our own thinking about the church ordinarily takes off from local gatherings, situations, and experiences, Paul's regular starting point was God's great plan for the church universal—perhaps four figures strong in his day, but more than ten figures strong (actually, two billion) in ours, not counting the saints who are in glory already. How then did he relate the various small congregations that he knew and served, several of which he had himself founded, to this larger reality in which he so fervently believed? His letters indicate. In Romans 12, explicitly addressing "everyone among you," he says: "As in one body we have many members" (the word means, body parts), "and the members do not all have the same function, so we, though many, are one body in Christ, and individually members of one another. Having gifts that differ according to the grace given to us, let us use them . . ." (Rom. 12:3–6). A list of capacities for ministry—gifts of speech, of service, and of lifestyle—then tumbles out in haphazard order, but all directed to the inner health of the Roman congregations. And again, writing to the church at Corinth, Paul says: "For just as the body is one and has many members, and all the members of the body, though many, are one body, so it is with Christ. . . . Now you are the body of Christ and individually members of it" (1 Cor. 12:12, 27). Paul is here applying to the local church the same theology that he developed for discussing the life of the church as the single global unit, in the way that he does in Ephesians 4:11–16, and this is very significant.

What it means is that for Paul the local church is called to be a miniature presentation of what the universal church is called to be. It is to be an outcrop, microcosm, sample, and specimen of the larger reality. It must see itself that way and act accordingly. Each local congregation must understand itself as a subset of the one global fellowship, a small-scale embodiment of that fellowship's life for all to see. And it is first and foremost by being a worthy embodiment that each such gathering brings glory to God.

From the human standpoint, the local church is a group of believers who band together to meet on a regular basis and do all the things that, according to the New Testament, the church does—praise and pray together, maintain ministry of the Word and sacraments, practice pastoral care and pastoral discipline toward each other, give and help where there is need, and reach out with the gospel to the neighborhood and beyond. Every-member ministry, in which all the gifts that God gives are put to work, is part of the ideal. At the same time, it is basic to the New Testament pattern that there be one or more servant leaders for each congregation with a stated role of preaching, teaching, and paternal oversight, and with personal responsibility both to the congregation and to God for faithfulness in that task. This shepherding ministry of leadership and coordination is essential for congregational health and strength.

This, with all the rest of what we have said so far, establishes the frame of reference and directly sets the stage for what now becomes the center of our attention, namely, Anglicanism today. May I say: I hope that non-Anglicans will not bypass the next few pages, though I know that in some quarters anti-Anglican sentiment runs high. The problems of Anglicanism today resurface in other church contexts, and all evangelicals will, I believe, gain wisdom and help for godly congregational life by thinking these problems through in their Anglican form.

ANGLICANISM

What is Anglicanism? Basically, it is the way of being and doing church that was shaped in England in the sixteenth century, as one of the fruits of Western Europe's Reformation. Two key planks in the Anglican platform at that time were submission to the authority of Holy Scripture as "God's Word written," to quote Article 20, and acceptance of the doctrine of the Thirty-Nine Articles of 1563, with their stress on justification through Christ alone by faith alone and on salvation by grace alone. The Church of England was and is a federation of some ten thousand parishes, organized into episcopally led dioceses divided into two provinces, with the archbishop of Canterbury as the prime primate. It is unique in being established by law as the church of the nation.

Wales, Scotland, and Ireland are separate provinces, each smaller than their English counterparts. By contrast, the United States is one huge province geographically, and so is Canada. Devoted missionary work has birthed further self-governing provinces all round the world. The Anglican Communion, that is, the association of all these provinces together, has about a thousand bishops and eighty million members. What marks the Communion out and gives it a sense of identity distinct from that of other Protestant church families is, first, its worship style, rooted in or at least developed from the Reformation/Restoration Prayer Books of 1549, 1552, and 1662, and, second, its retention of bishops as the head persons of dioceses. What has kept it together thus far is a sense of the unique richness of its heritage, plus goodwill all round. Whether, or in what form, it can stay together in light of its current internal cleavages is, as of now, anyone's guess.

There have long been different types of Anglicans with divergent opinions on many matters, but in the past all the groups have characteristically shown a strong sense of Christian and historical proportion, of mutual respect, and of the need for credible outward expression of the church's given unity in Christ. This mind-set has made Anglicans down the centuries into ecumenical pioneers. Until recently it was understood that Anglicans sought consensus, waited for each other, and took no action that might marginalize or disfranchise any body of responsible Anglican opinion. It is the current change at this point that threatens the togetherness of the Anglican Communion. A damn-your-eyes habit of mind has taken over in certain quarters, and it is apparent that the end is not yet.

What are *bishops*? Clergy leaders appointed to manage dioceses. Thereby hangs a tale that, since it is often beclouded with bafflegab, I shall try to tell in the simplest terms possible.

In the New Testament, members of the appointed groups of

leaders in local churches are called both elders (presbyters, as in Jewish synagogues) and bishops (Greek, *episkopoi*, a functional word meaning those who oversee others).

By the early second century, however, in most churches if not all, the title of bishop was being reserved for the leadership group's leader. This was a natural development—though we know nothing of how it actually happened—for leaderless groups tend to drift, and having a group leader (team captain, as we might say) always makes sense.

Then in the early fourth century, as part of his policy to make Christianity the most favored religion, Constantine divided the empire into administrative areas called dioceses for bishops to run as civil governors (praetors) ran Rome's provinces. The bishop of the major city in each diocese became the area manager, overseeing all clergy and congregations within his jurisdiction as the chief disciplinary officer of the diocese. To keep out heretical bishops, who were very much part of the fourth-century scene, the rule was established that each bishop's jurisdiction in his own diocese was exclusive. With the authority of custom, this rule still holds wherever bishops are found, and some treat it as unchangeable, like the laws of the Medes and Persians. Custom, of course, regularly imposes a false sense of permanence. But change here is now becoming imperative, as we shall shortly see.

In the Middle Ages the belief developed that bishops were carriers and transmitters of an apostolic commission, stemming from Jesus himself, without which neither the Episcopal ordination of priests nor the sacraments that priests administered would be valid—that is, used as a channel of grace by God. Roman Catholicism still maintains this concept of apostolic succession, and so do some Anglicans, but it is no part of Anglicanism's self-definition, and John Wesley once wrote of it as "a fable that no man ever did or could prove."

During the Middle Ages, diocesan bishops became deeply

involved in civil as well as ecclesiastical administration, and when England's new Prayer Book ordinal of 1549 defined and highlighted the spiritual tasks of bishops, this political involvement did not cease. To this day English bishops are appointed by the prime minister on the monarch's behalf, as so many servants of the crown. The post-Reformation history of the English episcopate shows ongoing oscillation between political commitments (like sitting in the House of Lords during its sessions); pastoral leadership as preacher, teacher, ordainer, confirmer, counselor of clergy, and reconciler of parish wars; and church administration (choosing, ordaining, appointing, licensing, and disciplining clergy, plus organizing, strategizing, fundraising, and so on, as need has required), with each bishop pursuing his personal priorities within this varied frame of activity. Such, apart from politics, has been the pattern of episcopacy outside England too. Of necessity, a great deal of discretionary power goes with the bishop's job. How could it be done otherwise? So power becomes integral to the idea of the bishop in people's minds, including sometimes the minds of bishops themselves.

Is this setup biblical? If you mean, is it mandated or exemplified in the Bible, the answer is no, although its ancestry and reflection of the ministry performed by the apostles and their deputies, as we see it in the Pastoral Epistles in particular, is clear. But if you mean, does it express New Testament principles and priorities regarding the local church's life, and does it meet the New Testament requirement that everything in the church be geared for edification, then the answer is surely yes, and the incidence of bad bishops from time to time does not invalidate that answer. Episcopal ministry in idea, if not always in reality, embodies the connectional link between congregations that our given unity in Christ demands, and can provide unifying leadership for the diocese, just as the consultations of the House of Bishops should do for the province, and as the primates' meetings should do for the Anglican Communion as a whole. The demands of Anglican-defined Episcopal office, if taken seriously, will doubtless drain the energy of its occupants, but those they lead will be enriched, so that their dioceses will have every reason to thank God for them.

But—and this is a big "but"—if Anglican dioceses are to be blessed with a steady flow of bishops of this kind, two conditions have to be met. Bishops must be well chosen and well monitored by those they lead; and in saying this I have laypeople particularly in view. Many dioceses in many places languish for lack of responsible, discerning Episcopal elections and a set pattern of realistic Episcopal accountability. As regards the former, voters regularly treat concern for doctrinal faithfulness as a minor thing and allow other factors to decide their choice. As regards the latter, mutual accountability enters into all healthy Christian relationships without exception, and the effect of its absence is ordinarily, to say the least, less than happy, so that to exempt bishops from it does no favor either to them or to us. What then is the problem here? Lay apathy, I am afraid, which lets bishops, once in place, do pretty much whatever they want to do, without challenge. This is to say in effect that Anglican episcopacy all the world over is at this point an underdeveloped institution, and that until change comes, Anglican congregations are more likely than not to suffer from this fact.

THE WORLDLINESS VIRUS

The New Testament teaches us to think of the world as the human community organized explicitly without God and implicitly against God, as the Devil leads, and to define worldliness as conformity to the world's ways. Anglicanism, by reason of its historic involvement with national community life in so many places, is constantly vulnerable to worldly influences, which operate as do viruses both in the human bloodstream and in the electronic brains of computers: infecting, damaging, and threatening to destroy the entire system. A perfect, large-scale instance of this is the current inclination of leaders in what I have been calling Old Western Anglicanism—that is, Anglican dioceses and provinces in Britain, North America, and Australasia—to rate gay unions under certain conditions as a form of holiness, parallel to marriage and pleasing to God. This reflects, of course, the affirmative attitude toward homosexual behavior that has come to mark secular society in the countries mentioned. We label this view, as its own adherents do, *liberal*, and the opposite view *conservative*, or, better, *conservationist*, since it treats the biblical condemnation of homosexual activity as revealed truth from God, permanently valid and thus to be adhered to as one element in faithful discipleship to Jesus Christ.

Behind this direct parting of the ways lie two factors, both of which are about half a century old. The first factor is a reconceiving of the task of Christian mission as simply speaking and modelling love and justice to all the world in terms that the secular community will immediately recognize and endorse as matching its own highest ideals. The second factor is the decriminalizing of homosexual behavior throughout the English-speaking world, so that gay identities, values, and goals may now be paraded in public without restriction or inhibition. And the world presses the church similarly to sanction homosexual relationships. The Anglican Communion, which maintained the conservationist position unambiguously as recently as the Lambeth Conference of 1998, is currently at odds over this question and over the clashing views of biblical authority that the rival positions entail. Interprovincial and intradiocesan fellowship has suffered, realignments involving overlapping jurisdictions has taken place, and arrangements to found a new North American province are now under way. It is a sorry scene and one of which the worldliness virus is a direct cause.

It has been said, mainly by persons who desire to lead all of Anglicanism along the liberal path, that this difference of opinion, however distressing, should not be seen as church dividing, that is, as warranting withdrawals, realignments, and any restricting or restructuring of Anglicanism's present internal communion.

Space does not permit me to discuss that thesis here, but I must at once point out that any church body that deliberately and publicly embraces approval of gay behavior in any form *prima facie* undercuts its own claim to be (1) *holy*, in biblical terms, at least in the sexual realm; (2) *catholic*, since this is a minority view, which Roman Catholicism, Eastern Orthodoxy, and most of the Protestant world see as heretical; (3) *apostolic*, since Paul specifically rules out homosexual relationships in all forms as incompatible with kingdom-of-God living. A church body that lends approval to gay behavior also renders empty any claim to be part of the church that is *one*, in that this church body has now itself disrupted God-given Christian unity.

SCHISM

This paradoxical claim that sanctioning gay lifestyles is not itself divisive leads us to the subject of schism, on which we need now to focus.

The word *schism*, a Greek word originally, means a division or split of some kind. It has a long history in the church as a heavy-duty term of censure, that is, as a label for what is seen as causeless, needless, unwarranted, and unjustifiable dividing of the church visible here on earth. As we have already said, unity in Christ through union with Christ is God's gift to all believers and is a reality that the church is under obligation to display to the world every way it can. Schism is irresponsible disrupting of a unit of the worldwide church of Christ and has always been perceived as a sinful breach of the shared conviction and consensual love that should bind together all members of that unit in full fellowship with each other. This diagnosis applies whether the unit that splits is a single congregation or a denominational group of congregations or a diocese or province, Anglican or otherwise. Those accused of schism always justify their withdrawal by claiming that the unit's unfaithfulness to Christ and the Bible drove them to it, making separation the only course of action by which they could preserve their own faithfulness, and keep clear of the spiritual betrayal into which the unit had fallen. Accusations of schism regularly fly both ways, one group accusing the other of causing division by their separation and the other protesting the undermining of true Christianity that was the cause of their conviction that they had to withdraw. The dictum that the real schismatic is not necessarily the one who separates but the one who causes the separation has a long history, as of course does the cynical strategy, give a dog a bad name and hang it.

Here are two historical illustrations of the reality of schism:

1. When the Donatists had withdrawn from the catholic church in the fourth century, judging it irremediably defiled by still accepting leaders who under persecution had let it seem they were renouncing their faith, Augustine argued that they were cutting their own throats spiritually by refusing to exercise forgiving love. His point was eventually taken, and the Donatists rejoined the catholic Christian communion. Here doctrine was not the issue, only discipline.

2. When in the sixteenth century papal officialdom accused the Reformers and their followers of schism because they had abandoned Rome's jurisdiction, the comeback was that Rome's Christianity had become so misshapen and its errors about salvation so deeply rooted, that Rome had in effect unchurched itself, and withdrawal was therefore necessary in order to put the church, country by country, back in shape again in its faith and life. Today, the language of schism is hardly heard on either side of this divide; Roman Catholic leaders and their conservationist Protestant counterparts hail each other as separated brethren and cooperate in various theological enterprises aimed at convergence and consensus. But it is well to remember that the differences regarding belief and behavior are still too great to allow any form of reunion, at least by biblical standards. The Reformation disagreements about the infallibility and authority of the church and about the way of salvation divide us still.

Recently, the phrase *internal schism* has been coined to describe situations in which, without actual separation, warring groups within the same church structure restrict church communion in some way. An example of this was the action of almost a hundred members of the 2002 synod of the diocese of New Westminster, who, when the bishop responded favorably to the synod's majority request that he initiate the blessing of same-sex unions, declared themselves out of communion with him and the synod till this decision was rescinded, and walked out to show that they meant what they said. Following this, the congregations that they represented withheld their diocesan apportionments for the time being, on the ground that they could not in good conscience subsidize sin, while they sought direct dialogue with the diocese regarding the issue itself (a request that unhappily was not granted). Other cases of internal schism beginning with protest over this same matter have since surfaced in various parts of North America.

ORIENTATION

Anglicans in Canada, willy-nilly, must face the question of how to position themselves in the situation that has now developed, whereby a new province of orthodox faith, territorially overlapping both the Anglican Church of Canada (ACC) and the Episcopal Church in the United States (TEC), has been formed. The first members of the Anglican Church in North America (ACNA) are the one hundred thousand refugees, if we may so call them, whose dioceses or provinces have embraced the view that well-meant gay unions are a mode of holiness parallel to marriage and should be blessed accordingly and, by rejecting their conscientious opposition to this, have in effect squeezed them out. Both provinces denounce the new move on the grounds that overlapping Episcopal jurisdictions contravene historic catholic practice, and they are stone-deaf to the argument that when whole dioceses, led by their bishops, go off the rails, alternative jurisdiction becomes a necessity. So although the new venture has been welcomed by the GAFCON group of primates (that is, those present at the Global Anglican Future Conference, held in Jerusalem in

June 2008), and although the archbishop of Canterbury has declined a request to declare himself out of communion with those who are realigning, both the Canadian and American provinces refuse so far to think or speak well of what is being done. In these circumstances, all faithful Anglicans must ask themselves, what ought I to do now for the furthering of the true gospel, the good of tomorrow's church and the worldwide Christian mission, and the glory of God the Father, the Son, and the Holy Spirit?

Four key considerations bear on this question.

1. The presenting issue (the conflicting evaluations of homosexual partnerships) is a major matter, for three reasons. (a) The question is practical, not just theoretical. Whereas previous doctrinal differences within Anglicanism have all been matters of opinion that scarcely touched on actual conduct except perhaps at a motivational level, this contention seeks to rehabilitate and celebrate as virtue behavior that Scripture identifies, in black and white as it were, as sin (Lev. 18:22; 20:13; Rom. 1:26–27; 1 Cor. 6:9–11; 1 Tim. 1:8–10). (b) Our salvation itself is directly involved, for we find Paul warning his readers that homosexual behavior bars the way to the kingdom of God, and in the next breath joyfully celebrating the fact that the Holy Spirit had enabled Corinthian believers to break their own homosexual habits, which we know were much encouraged by the Corinthian culture (see 1 Cor. 6:11). (c) Sex is an important aspect of our being (no one today will dispute that), and God's purpose for sex, over and above personal pleasure and mutual bonding, is, as it always was, procreation, the continuance of the human race (Gen. 1:28). To indulge sexual desire in a way that makes sex barren is, quite simply, defying the divine purpose.

2. If the testimony of Scripture can be trusted (and it can!), Jesus Christ the Lord, the God-man, as divine as his Father and as human as we are, loves the church and has invested himself to a breathtaking degree in the program of redeeming her and leading her, as his bride, to a perfection of holiness that matches what he himself

modelled here on earth. And if Scripture can further be trusted, Paul and his fellow-apostles had the mind of Christ, so that when they taught, Christ taught through them, and what they taught was his teaching. But if that is so, then those who would sanction gay unions contradict Christ.

3. Pastoral care of fellow-believers is every Christian's business. Certainly, the clergy must lead here; they are explicitly charged to teach, guard, nurture, and equip the flock, keeping them in order and setting them to work. But serving, helping, watching over, and caring for others is not just the clergy's job; it is a universal Christian obligation. All of us, then, must clear our minds as to what constitutes pastoral care in the church, and specifically pastoral care of persons who experience same-sex attraction. Should we affirm and support them as they enter into physical partnerships? Is this how the *agape* love that seeks their welfare is to be expressed? Or does *agape* love require us rather to affirm and support them by forming bonds of friendship with them and within those bonds seeking to fortify them against yielding to the urgings that they have to live with? The two strategies are exclusive of each other; there is no fence here for anyone to sit on. Before God, clergy and laity alike have to make up their minds. And if the testimony of Scripture is really trusted, this will not prove hard to do.

4. The forming of the new, biblically based province (the Anglican Church in North America) raises the question of who, besides the ecclesiastical refugees mentioned above, should join it, and when. Certainly, it has been born in a great wave of enthusiasm, and, equally certainly, it will carry great hopes for the future, whereas the ACC and TEC are currently generating only great fears. But any active recruiting from ACC or TEC—sheep stealing, that is—would itself be slippage toward schism and must not happen. It is true that the presence of unacceptable and seemingly incurable lapses, doctrinally and ethically, in these provinces sets Christians free to look for a more congenial spiritual home, where

the true reality of the one church as God sees and knows it is better expressed. But existing ministry obligations of one sort or another may well demand that, for the present, however unhappily, one stays where one is. In any case, decisions to change one's congregation, and in this case one's jurisdiction also, should not be made hastily or without consultation and prayer, lest one's enthusiasm override one's discernment and judgment. The grass on the other side of the fence always looks greener, and it has often been said that any who think they have found a perfect church should not join it, since they would spoil it. The safe path is to be quick to pray but slow to move; and we must never lose sight of the fact that a renewing, reviving visitation of the Holy Spirit, such as I imagine my readers are already praying for, can remove roadblocks in a very remarkable way. The bottom line is that all should seek God's guidance as to what they should do with reference to the new arrival, and meantime seek to show goodwill and *agape* love to all parties. And if we become sure that God is directing us to withdraw and realign, then to follow the rule John Wesley made for members of his Methodist societies: If you must leave, go out quietly.

May God in his wisdom and mercy guide us all.

Almighty and everlasting God, by whose Spirit the whole body of the Church is governed and sanctified; Receive our supplications and prayers, which we offer before thee for all estates of men in thy holy Church, that every member of the same, in his vocation and ministry, may truly and godly serve thee; through our Lord and Savior Jesus Christ. (Second Good Friday collect, Book of Common Prayer, 1962, Canada)

QUESTIONS FOR STUDY AND DISCUSSION

1. How would you demonstrate the central place of the church in the saving purpose of God?
2. What ministry has God given you in your local congregation?
3. How should local churches relate to each other?

4. What do you see as the major elements in the Anglican heritage? What value do you set on them?
5. How would you meet the criticism that forming a new Anglican province in territory where an Anglican presence already exists is a schismatic act?
6. What are the proper priorities of a local evangelical congregation?
7. How should we care for fellow-worshippers in the congregations of which we are part?

6

TAKING THE HOLY
SPIRIT SERIOUSLY

PENTECOST

"It's a very important day," chirruped the disc jockey as he looked ahead to May 11, 2008. "It's Mother's Day!" Well, so it was, and who would wish to deny its importance as such? But it was also Pentecost Sunday, and that aspect of its importance was not mentioned at all. Isn't Pentecost very important, after all? To judge by the way many churches and Christians behave at Pentecost, not very. But are they right to make so little of it, treating it as hardly different from any other Sunday? I do not think they are, and I want to tell you why.

Pentecost, or Whitsunday as it used to be called, looks back to the momentous morning when Jesus's disciples, meeting for prayer, heard the roar of a tornado, saw flames shoot down from the ceiling onto each person's head, and found their mouths working and sounds coming out that later proved to be languages they had never learned. Running out onto the street, they found that some bystanders visiting Jerusalem from far away were hearing the disciples proclaim the dying, rising, and reign of Jesus in their own local tongues. The disciples gathered round Peter as, at the top of his voice, with an authority and clarity that he had never before shown or known, he preached the good news of Jesus (probably in Greek, the *lingua franca* of the Roman world and of the international Jewish community). And they watched, amazed, as some three thousand hearers embraced Peter's message, professed their repentance, lined up for baptism, and threw in their lot with the fellowship of the faithful, Jesus's tongues-speaking disciples, the nucleus of the new community.

Pentecost was the day of the Spirit's *outpouring*. (Joel's, Peter's, and Luke's chosen wording, "pour[ed] out"—Acts 2:17, 33—implies overwhelming abundance, as water flows in a cloudburst or when a river bursts its banks.) It was the birthday of the church as we know it (that is, as a company of believers in Jesus, the international society of the born again). And in God's great scheme of salvation this was as epoch-making an event as was the incarnation of the Son of God, which we celebrate each Christmas, and his sin-bearing death and life-imparting resurrection, which we celebrate every Holy Week and Easter. Each was an event that changed the world, by reason of the new reality that it added.

Yet Pentecost does not catch the imagination or call forth the major commemorative action of God's people in the way that Christmas and Easter do. Why is that? Focusing now specifically on the Anglican Communion, about which I can speak with some confidence, I answer my question thus: Pentecost does not mean much to us because, speaking generally, the ministry of the Holy Spirit does not bulk large in either our thinking or our living. And that is something that urgently needs to change.

MINUS THE SPIRIT

What we have in the church in the absence of a vivid and challenging awareness of what the Holy Spirit does to us and through us is one or more of the following travesties of Christianity:

- *Institutionalism*, for which the top priorities are the upkeep of church buildings; the regular performing of the worship services; the organization, administration, and stability of the congregation, the diocese, and the global Anglican Communion; and an unwillingness to rock the Anglican boat locally, nationally, or internationally.

- *Formalism*, for which the top priorities are church attendance; correct behavior during the public praise, prayer, and
  preaching; correct behavior out of church; a personal routine,
  skimpy perhaps, of daily prayers; and a strong confidence that
  going through these motions brings spiritual stature and so
  pleases God.
- *Moralism*, for which the top priority is conforming to what is
  understood as the code of Christ, in the belief that this is the
  essence of Christianity and the way of salvation.
- *Traditionalism*, for which the top priority is preserving the
  comfort zone of time-honored old paths in church life, and
  fighting for them against all would-be revisionists.

There are, to be sure, grains of truth and wisdom in all these
attitudes. Real Christians do share deeply in church life and care
deeply about its quality. They do discipline themselves to pray, both
privately and publicly. They know that from one standpoint the
Christian life is a life of prayer, and that keeping in touch with God
is its very essence. They know that they are called to be Christlike
in obeying God's laws, and they labor to do their best, though at
the same time they know they are sinners who constantly fall short
and who can only live by being constantly forgiven. And they know
that the church's heritage is to be valued, for wisdom from the Holy
Spirit permeates it, whatever else it may contain.

The problem with the attitudes listed is simply that they bypass
the gospel, marginalizing the ministry of our Lord and Savior Jesus
Christ and with it the reality of life in and with Christ through the
Holy Spirit—the life of worshipping, praying, moving, and ministering "in" the Spirit, as the New Testament often puts it. (What
a weight of truth that little word "in" carries when so used!)
This bypassing, however, means that they miss the real heart of
Christianity; to adapt words from Paul, they have the outward form
of godliness without its inward power.

When I was a theological student, nearly two generations ago, discerning teachers used to lament the marginalizing of the Holy Spirit, calling him the displaced person of the Godhead and the Cinderella of theology. Since those days, a significant minority of Anglicans and others have been impacted by the charismatic movement, with its insistence that we must be open to God and uninhibited in our expression of praise, gratitude, joy, hope, confidence, and excitement Christ-ward. Much of this was in fact a recovery of the spiritual liveliness that had marked the seventeenth-century Puritans and the eighteenth-century evangelicals, though (shall we say) differently orchestrated, in a different key, and with certain changed emphases. Distinctive to the charismatic movement was the Pentecostal idea that God is restoring in the modern church most if not all of the apostolic sign gifts (prophecy, tongues and interpretation, and healing), plus Spirit baptism with tongues, as on Pentecost morning—a claim that many Christians, like this writer, find dubious. When this dogma is deleted, however, what remains is a renewing of something that Anglicans once knew, should never have lost, and today need to find once more—namely, the experience of being searched by the Holy Spirit through the Scriptures to learn our own deep need, and of being led hereby into a face-to-face relationship with Jesus Christ our Savior and our Lord, whom the Holy Spirit through the same Scriptures makes present to us.

PLUS THE SPIRIT

"Theology," said the fourth-century teacher Gregory, bishop of Nazianzus—who in his lifetime was hailed as "the theologian," just as Calvin was centuries later—"reaches maturity through additions." He was thinking, of course, of additions that reflect the progress of revelation in history. In Old Testament times, God proclaimed himself in his exclusive oneness, with only obscure hints at his intrinsic triunity, and faithful Israelite theology was monotheistic to the core. Through the witness of the incarnate Son to his relation with his Father, the plurality of persons within the divine unity was laid open, and the church spent its first several centuries augmenting Jewish theology by seeking appropriate agreed-upon ways to verbalize the Trinity and the incarnation. The book of Acts, which narrates Pentecost and its consequences, and with it the apostles' pastoral letters, set forth the ministry of the third divine person, the Holy Spirit, very fully, but prior to the Reformation era this topic was not explored in any detail. Since then, however, study of the Spirit (pneumatology, as it is called) has moved steadily forward, with John Calvin's *Institutes*, John Owen's *Pneumatologia*, and Abraham Kuyper's *Work of the Holy Spirit* being perhaps the highlights.

Now, therefore, standing on our predecessors' shoulders, let us take a good hard look at the biblical presentation of the Holy Spirit of God.

The Name of the Holy Spirit

In the Bible, God-given names are not just labels; they are revelations. Thus, Yahweh (Jehovah), God's covenant name for himself, which he told to Moses at the burning bush (Ex. 3:13–15), is short for a Hebrew phrase meaning "I am (and/or, will be) what (and/or, who) I am (and/or, will be)," which declared his eternal, self-sustaining sovereignty in the face of a hostile and seemingly chaotic world. And when Jesus named the one he loved and served as "Father," that word declared authoritative love, care, direction, provision, and protection—fatherhood to perfection, as we might say. Jesus's own human name, given him by angels (Matt. 1:21; Luke 1:31), the Greek form of the Hebrew Joshua, which means "God is Savior," was a defining declaration of his ministry: "You shall call his name Jesus, for he shall save his people from their sins." "Holy Spirit" is also a declaratory revelation. "Holy," carrying the basic idea of separateness, signifies those qualities in God that set him in contrast with us, namely, transcendent majesty and full moral purity—qualities that can make him awesome, indeed fearsome, to encounter, as Isaiah found (Isa. 6:5), and as all impenitent humans will one day find also (Rom. 2:5–16; Rev. 6:13–17). "Spirit" (Hebrew, *ruach*; Greek, *pneuma*) carries the basic idea of wind blowing, as in a storm, or breath puffed out, as when extinguishing a candle, and so signifies divine power in energetic action. The name thus declares the reality of omnipotence at work, creating, controlling, transforming, and moving out in retributive judgment.

The Personhood of the Holy Spirit

There are about a hundred references to the Spirit in the Old Testament, and each time the phrase is "the (holy) Spirit of God (the Lord)" or "his (your) (holy) Spirit." The thought on each occasion is of the powerful resources that God possesses and deploys, as when Scripture speaks of the eyes, or hand, or arm of the Lord. There is, however, no suggestion as yet of the Spirit being a distinct person. From all eternity he was so, of course, but this was not made known till Christ came. But in Jesus's last talk to his disciples before his betrayal, the Spirit's separate personhood was made unambiguously clear.

> I will ask the Father, and he will give you another Helper, to be with you forever, even the Spirit of truth . . . .
>
> The Helper, the Holy Spirit, whom the Father will send in my name, he will teach you all things and bring to your remembrance all that I have said to you. (John 14:16–17, 26)

> It is to your advantage that I go away, for if I do not go away, the Helper will not come to you. But if I go, I will send him to you. And when he comes, he will convict the world concerning sin and righteousness and judgment . . . . When the Spirit of truth comes, he will guide you into all the truth, for he will not speak on his own authority, but whatever he hears he will speak . . . . He will glorify me, for he will take what is mine and declare it to you. (John 16:7–8, 13–14)

The Spirit is here said to speak, teach, witness, guide, declare, and convince. He is named a "Helper," that is, a *paraclētos*, which word can mean a comforter in the sense of a strengthener, an encourager, an advocate, and a supporter. He is presented as "another [a second] Helper," in Jesus's place—evidently, then, one who exists on the same footing and in the same order of reality as Jesus himself. Testimony to the divine personhood of the Holy Spirit could hardly be clearer. The accounts of the Spirit's ministry in the history that Acts records and Paul's references to the Spirit interceding for us and sometimes being grieved by us (Rom. 8:26–27; Eph. 4:30) further confirm this testimony. The Holy Spirit is as truly a divine person as are the Father and the Savior.

THE SPIRIT AT WORK
In the Old Testament we read of the Holy Spirit

- sharing in the creation of this world order and in control of what we call its natural and historical processes (Gen. 1:2; Ps. 104:29–30; Isa. 34:16);
- revealing God's truth and will to his messengers by both direct communication and the wisdom of distilled insight (Num. 24:2; 2 Sam. 23:2; 1 Chron. 12:18; 2 Chron. 15:1; Neh. 9:30; Job 32:8; Isa. 61:1–4; Ezek. 2:2; 11:24; 37:1; Mic. 3:8; Zech. 7:12), and teaching God's people through these revelations the way of faithfulness and fruitfulness (Neh. 9:20; Ps. 143:10; Isa. 48:16; 63:10–14);
- eliciting personal response to God—knowledge of God in the Bible's own sense of that phrase—in the form of faith, repentance, hope, joy, obedience, holiness, openness to God's instruction and direction, and fellowship with him through praise and prayer (Pss. 51:10–12, etc.; Isa. 11:2; 44:3; Ezek. 11:19; 36:25–27; 37:14; 39:29; Joel 2:28–29; Zech. 12:10);
- equipping individuals for service, both as community leaders and as community craftsmen (Gen. 41:38, Joseph; Ex. 31:1–11, 35:30–35, Bezalel and Oholiab; Num. 11:17, Moses; 11:16–29,

seventy elders; 27:18, Joshua; Judg. 3:7–10, Othniel; 6:34, Gideon; 11:29, Jephthah; 13:25, 14:19, 15:14, Samson; 1 Sam. 10:10, 11:6, see also 19:20–23, Saul; 16:13, David; 2 Kings 2:9–15, Elijah and Elisha; Isa. 11:1–5, 42:1–4, the Messiah; Hag. 2:5 and Zech. 4:6, temple builders).

The New Testament builds on all this, but expands much of it by relating it directly, on the one hand, to the person and work of the incarnate, crucified, risen, ascended, and glorified Son of God and, on the other hand, to the persons who are brought by the Spirit through faith in Christ into union and communion with Jesus in his risen life.

The Holy Spirit and Jesus Christ the Savior

The Spirit, whose creative power effected the conception of Jesus in Mary's womb (Luke 1:35), was with and within the incarnate Son throughout his life on earth. He disclosed his presence to Jesus, to John, and perhaps to others by the apparition of the dove at Jesus's baptism (Matt. 3:16–17; John 1:32–33), which convinced John that "this is he who baptizes with the Holy Spirit." The Spirit bearer, so John was told, would in due course be the Spirit giver. The Spirit at once led Jesus into the wilderness "to be tempted by the devil" (Matt. 4:1); he participated in all the Savior's ministry (Luke 4:14), empowering his miracles (Matt. 12:28), prompting his joy (Luke 10:21), and sustaining him through the agony of Gethsemane for the greater agony of his atoning death (Heb. 9:14). As we Christians are upheld by the Holy Spirit in the life that we live with God and for God, so was our Savior before us. As we live in a simultaneous relationship with the Father, the Son, and the Holy Spirit, who are always together and never apart from each other, so were the Father and the Spirit together with the Son when he was on earth, as they are still and always will be.

The Holy Spirit and Those Whom Jesus Christ Saves

The perspective here is fixed by Jesus's own affirmation, "He will glorify me, for he will take what is mine and declare it to you" (John 16:14). As the Son's prime goal in all his dealings with our sinful race was and is always the Father's glory—that is, that the Father be praised for the revealed praiseworthiness of his deeds, so the Holy Spirit's prime goal in his ministry to us who become Christians was and is always the Savior's glory—that is, praise for the love and compassion, wisdom and humility, faithfulness and endurance of pain, and every other virtue that Jesus showed as he lived, died, lived again, and lives still, for the fulfilling of the divine saving purpose toward us. From this standpoint the Spirit's ongoing ministry may be compared to a floodlight trained on a building of grandeur, picking out all the manifold details of its dignity and beauty. Highlighting Christ for praise purposes is central in all aspects of the Spirit's ministry to Christian people.

TEACHER AND TRANSFORMER

Within this frame, the Spirit ministers to us in the following main ways:

First and fundamentally, he *teaches us* the truth about God—his being, his ways, his plans, his goodness and grace, and his will for our lives. He does this through the apostolic witness to Christ (John 17:20), which we have written in the books of the New Testament for our permanent use. These books are to be read as organically one with the Jewish Scriptures, which we call the Old Testament. As the Spirit is in a real sense the author of all these Scriptures, so in a real sense he now acts as their interpreter, constantly leading us into deeper understanding of their message and application to us than we had before (2 Tim. 3:15–17; Heb. 3:7–11; 10:15–17; 2 Pet. 1:19–21). Here, again, following Christ's own focus on the Old Testament as pointing to himself (Luke 24:27, 44; John 5:39), the Spirit unfolds an understanding to us that glorifies Jesus the Lord.

Second, the Spirit *renews our hearts*, that is, the inner core of each Christian's being, the source of all the thoughts, desires, motives, purposes, creative urgings, ambitions, concerns, convictions, reactions, relational attitudes, loves, hates, hopes, fears, and whatever else contributes, in personality terms, to making us the people that we are. Whereas, before our contact with Christ, our hearts were naturally bent on self-service and self-aggrandizement and so were bent in another sense—bent out of true in terms of what God made us for—the Spirit, using the Word of God as both scalpel and exercise machine, straightens out our inner crookedness and energizes us for spiritual understanding, spiritual response to God, and spiritual, love-led, Christlike, God-honoring behavior as our lifestyle henceforth.

The New Testament message in sum is like an ellipse, that is, an oval outline, with two focal points. The first focal point is the person, place, and past, present, and predicted work of Jesus Christ, Son of God and Son of Man, Savior, Lord, and Friend, lion of Judah and lamb of God, who is to be glorified by angels and humans for all eternity. The second focal point is the momentous transformation that takes place in the lives of those whom Jesus saves—from the initial renewal of our heart, through the ongoing remaking of our character in Christ's moral image by the Spirit who now indwells each of us, to the final full conforming of us as perfected souls in resurrection bodies to our exalted Lord, in whose company we shall live forever. Linking these two focal points is the active agency of the Spirit, who works the change in us by creating and sustaining union between us and our risen Lord, such that the new life that we live is at the same time Jesus Christ living his resurrection life in us and through us. The books of the New Testament—Christ and his apostles, that is—frequently tell us that Christians live "in" Christ, and Christ lives "in" us; what has just been said is what is meant.

In relation to our lives, this momentous inner renewal is pictured by Jesus (John 3:3–8), James (1:18), Peter (1 Pet. 1:23), and John (1 John 2:29–3:9; 5:1, 4, 18) as a *new birth* that involves the implanting in us of God's imperishable "seed." This "seed," the carrier of life, is an image for a triggering, energizing, transforming divine force. The thought is of being made radically and permanently different from what we were, on the inside first and then in the outward expression of a changed heart. Theologians call this work of the Spirit regeneration. Jesus told Jewish pundit Nicodemus that without being born again in this way none can see or enter the kingdom of God, and he added that persons so born would be beyond the comprehension of others, just as whence and where the whirling wind comes and goes are matters beyond our own comprehension. Perceptually and motivationally, Christians find that new birth by the Spirit's action supernaturalizes their whole life. They live in a new dimension, with God, for God, under God, by the power of God; and the watching world, which does not know God, cannot tell what it is that makes them tick. Because they are no longer spiritually blind, deaf, and indeed dead (that is, utterly unresponsive to God; see 2 Cor. 4:4; Eph. 2:1–7; 4:17–24), their heart's desire is now to find and follow a Christ-centered, God-honoring way of life. But that takes them out of the world's sphere of thought, even as they continue in the world, seeking to serve it according to what they see as its real needs. So we should not be surprised that the world cannot make them out and often resents them for their supposed superiority complex.

Third, following on from what has just been said, the Spirit *changes our lives*; for he moves us along the path of *faith* and *repentance* as principles of daily functioning. While these two realities are often thought of separately, they belong together, being two aspects of the same thing, namely, *turning to God*, as we shall now see.

Faith begins as the realization, which the Holy Spirit generates, that God our Creator, in whose hands we always are and by whom our destiny will finally be decided, is really real, and that Jesus

Christ the Savior, once crucified and now glorified, who invites us to himself for salvation, is really real too. Faith blossoms into a response of belief and trust, credence and commitment, to the grace of God in the apostolic gospel, the promises of God in the Bible, and the personal approach to us through the Spirit's agency of the Son of God himself. Faith is a whole-souled response to this threefold manifesting of mercy. The response combines intellectual acceptance, emotional embrace, and resolute submission in a reordered life pattern that puts us always at our Savior's service as his dependants and disciples. *Hope* then is faith looking ahead by the light of God's promises, *joy* is faith reflecting on its knowledge of the Savior and its prospect of eternal glory with him, and *repentance* is faith renouncing errors and shortcomings of the past.

Repentance means forsaking sin. So it is more than regret and remorse, though that is its usual starting point. It is an actual abandonment of what has been wrong in order to replace it by what is right. Recognizing that things we have done and habits we have formed are sin in God's sight, we say good-bye to them, asking forgiveness of them through the cross and seeking strength to leave them totally behind, even when we think that doing this is going to feel like cutting off one's hand or one's foot or gouging out one's eye (see Matt. 5:29–30; 18:8–9). The life of faith in Christ does not start until true repentance begins, and because, despite our best efforts, slippage into sin regularly recurs, true repentance needs to become a daily discipline. Christians live by being repeatedly forgiven, and we are forgiven, precisely, when we repent. This leads on to our next point.

Fourth, the Spirit *conforms us to Christ*—in character, that is. Jesus lived out love of God and love of neighbor, God's two great commands, to perfection, so becoming a model for us all. The born again begin their discipleship in a state of spiritual infancy, with their powers of discernment and self-discipline not yet fully developed, and sin within them, dethroned but not yet destroyed, still actively marauding and seeking to recover control of them. From this starting point, the born again are to grow up into Christlike maturity through the power of the Spirit sustaining their own conscious efforts to live as they should. The whole of this process is usually called sanctification. It involves being energized, on the one hand, to cultivate new habits of virtue and, on the other hand, to squeeze the life out of existing habits of vice. With regard to the latter process, Paul uses two vivid verbs, both of which signify putting something to death, and both of which have traditionally been rendered *mortify* (Rom. 6:13; Col. 3:5). With regard to the former process, what should be said is that virtues are supernaturally vivified and increasingly practiced through the vital power of the Spirit enabling us to be what otherwise we never could be. "Love, joy, peace, patience, kindness, goodness, faithfulness, gentleness, self-control," viewed as met together in a single character—the moral profile of Jesus, now reproduced in each of his loyal disciples—constitute, says Paul, "the fruit of the Spirit" (Gal. 5:22–25). To display such Spirit-wrought Christlikeness must ever be the Christian's positive goal—a goal that the Spirit, if not resisted but relied on, will powerfully help us to achieve.

DEATH TO SIN

Sin within is however a lifelong problem for believers. The root system of morning glory, the bindweed that fills hedges with trumpet-shaped white flowers that fade as the day moves on, is a sprawling tangle of interlinked tubers that is virtually impossible to clear away once it has taken hold. Similarly, the anti-God, anti-wisdom, anti-human drive that Scripture calls sin is hydra-headed and formidably tangled in its expression. Devious and deceptive to the last degree, sin, acting like a Satanic second self, keeps finding new ways of expressing itself in us. From Augustine to C. S. Lewis, with a great cloud of witnesses in between them confirming what they say, sin's essence has been diagnosed as pride, the craving always to seem right, always to get ahead, and always to end up on top; and pride, subtle and self-effacing, has countless ways of expressing itself in a person's life while remaining unnoticed by that person and conceal-ing its true viciousness from his or her view. Then, when we have detected, repudiated, and, temporarily at least, mortified one out-breaking form of pride, another will have emerged behind our back, so to speak—pride, perhaps, at our sensitiveness to sin and our zeal for mortification—so that the whole process must be gone through again, and again, and again—as long as life lasts. Hence a basic move in the war with sin must be to pray repeatedly:

> Search me, O God, and know my heart!
> Try me and know my thoughts!
> And see if there be any grievous way in me,
> and lead me in the way everlasting! (Ps. 139:23–24)

For holiness, like sin, starts in the heart, and actually advances only as it discerns and counters ungodly attitudes and desires lurk-ing there. In this connection, Jesus's words to the disciples who slept in Gethsemane take on a wider relevance: "Watch [stay awake and on guard] and pray that you may not enter into temptation" (Matt. 26:41). The Spirit's contribution in all this is to do the searching and make us aware of what he has found, to sustain our prayerful alert-ness to the pervasive forms of evil, to make us aware of each tempta-tion as it arises and before we fall victim to it, and to keep before our minds the costly, constraining, humbling, motivating love of Christ for us. Hereby he increases our desire to please the Lord by showing our gratitude to him every way we can, and he makes thoughts of careless, irresponsible disobedience to him increasingly abhorrent.

We need to be aware that age, health, and circumstances cause temptations to vary; some vanish, others mutate, some are replaced, others recur. The symptoms of self-centered pride, from self-pity through the various forms of self-assertion to self-blinded stub-bornness, are not the same in the young as in the middle-aged and elderly, nor are temptations themselves identical for the needy and marginalized, on the one hand, and the affluent and lionized, on the other. It is possible to enter into a new form of temptation under the illusion that temptation is now being left behind. So the battle for true godliness goes on in seemingly endless entanglements with the deceitfulness of sin.

John Wesley's questions to those who wished to join his Methodist fellowship groups (the "bands") included these two, which mark a two-stage advance in spiritual honesty: "Do you desire to be told of your faults? Do you desire to be told of all your faults, and that plain and home?" If we are serious in opening ourselves to the ministry of the Holy Spirit, this is what he will do for us, and by this means lead us on in the war with sin. But are we serious? For many in our churches, this question seems to hang in the air.

Much of the teaching that we have reviewed concerning the Holy Spirit's ministry to us as individuals comes from apostolic pastoral letters, which were addressed to local congregations and were centered, directly or indirectly, on the Holy Spirit in the church's corporate life. To round off our presentation, we must now move on to this.

CHURCH ALIVE

The thoughts and prayers of the apostle Paul, church-planting evangelist and pastor extraordinary, were largely dictated by his "daily . . . anxiety for all the churches" (2 Cor. 11:28)—those little worshipping fellowships, ten, twenty, thirty, fifty, perhaps eighty strong (that's a guess, but a sober one, I think) that had come into being through his own and others' preaching of the gospel. But when the time came for theology—that is, thinking God's revealed thoughts after him and learning to see things as God sees them—Paul viewed these churches as so many microcosms, outcrops, specimens, and samples of God's global covenant people, the divine family, the true Israel, the new human race, the international association of born-again believers. Moreover, he focused on them as so many miniature presentations of a single invisible yet potent reality of interconnected life and energy—namely, the one body of which Christ is the Head and director, and the one bride whose spiritual beautifier is Christ her Bridegroom (see Eph. 1:22–23; 5:25–32). This organic unity of God's people in, with, and through, as well as under, Christ was foreshadowed by the Lord himself when he said that he and his disciples are as vine and branches (John 15:1–8). As, now, the source of life to this one church of God is the risen Lord Jesus, so the ongoing flow of life through the union of each human unit with Christ and with each other in Christ is effected by the Holy Spirit.

Two pairs of key thoughts give shape and substance to Paul's thinking about all of this. The first pair are the church's *unity* and its *ministry*.

The Unity of the Church

It cannot be said too strongly that the true organic unity of God's church, that is, its oneness in Christ as God's global organism of spiritual life, is an existing, given, God-created fact, and that what fixes its boundary in each case is the presence or absence of faith and repentance, as described above. Analyzing "the unity of the Spirit," Paul writes, "There is one body and one Spirit . . . one hope . . . one Lord, one faith, one baptism, one God and Father of all" (Eph. 4:3–6). This means that the unity of the church embraces all believers—Protestant, Roman Catholic, and Orthodox—while paid-up church adherents everywhere who lack personal faith in Christ are still outside the church as God discerns it, however zealous for their own denomination they may be. This is a point that evangelicals have long used to highlight the distinction between the visible church (the church as it appears to us) and the invisible church (the church as God knows it).

The Ministry of the Church

In the human body the parts are different from each other (hands, feet, eyes; bones, muscles, blood; etc.), and so it is in the church, says Paul (1 Cor. 12:12–26). In both cases the diversity is for unified functioning. In the church, ministry, which means service, is precisely Christ serving his people, and the world with them, through the Spirit-prompted action of his human agents. The capacity for being used by the Lord Jesus in this way is called a gift, or manifestation, of the Holy Spirit in a person's life (1 Cor. 12:4–11; 1 Pet. 4:10–11). Everyone who is alive in Christ is called and equipped to be Christ's hand, foot, mouthpiece, smile, or whatever it may be, in loving service of others, and it is through every-member ministry that the body of Christ grows as planned (Eph. 4:11–16).

Apostolic thinking about ministry in the church follows two complementary lines. On the one hand, systematic teaching, leading in worship, discipling the faithful of all ages, disciplining the disorderly, keeping the peace, sustaining the sick, poor, and underprivileged, and motivating zeal in the congregation are constant pastoral tasks, for which competent persons should be appointed to serve as elders and deacons. On the other hand, gifts for service are given to every Christian (Rom. 12:4–8), and all gifts are given to be used, so each person's proper form of service must be found and fitted into the congregation's ongoing life; otherwise the Spirit will be quenched to a degree, and the growth of the church toward the stature of Christ will be obstructed. Ministry is to be a matter of both-and, not either-or; we do not all have the same ministry, but we are all in ministry together.

The second pair of key thoughts for Paul have to do with the local church's *morality* and *vitality*.

The Morality of the Church

Living under the lordship of Jesus as his disciples and counted as God's children—brothers and sisters of Jesus in the Father's royal family—Christians are called to live in humble, reverent holiness, both individually and corporately (1 Pet. 1:14–17). The royal family's lifestyle should always honor the monarch. The church is called to be "zealous for good works" (Titus 2:14). The Corinthian Christians had lapsed into quarrelsomeness, internal rivalry, toleration of the morally intolerable, and total inconsiderateness toward each other—pure unlove, as we might call it. Paul belabored them very hard for falling so very short and letting pride in their giftedness exclude the practice of love from their way of life.

The Vitality of the Church

Disciple-making outreach constitutes the church's marching orders (Matt. 28:19–20), and inward-looking inertia regarding this task is indefensible. Paul was glad to think of the Philippian church as "standing firm in one spirit, with one mind striving side by side for the faith of the gospel" and as "children of God without blemish in the midst of a crooked and twisted generation, among whom you shine as lights in the world, holding fast to the word of life" (Phil. 1:27; 2:15–16). Paul's gladness shows us that this is how every church ought to be.

CONCLUSION

The three basic truths about the Holy Spirit are as follows: (1) He is a divine person, the third within God's tripersonal being and a distinct participant with the Father and the Son in every divine action. The Holy Three always work together. (2) In the operational team that is God, the Spirit is, so to speak, the executive facilitator, through whose hands-on agency all tasks in creation and redemption are performed. (3) The mark of the entire biblical presentation of the Spirit is a certain indirectness, since it is either the Father or the Son, or simply God in his fullness, who is the focus of attention, never the Spirit himself in isolation. His executive role is a supportive one; his task, and his achievement, is always to exalt the Father and the Son.

Taking the Spirit seriously means embracing this perspective, thinking with conscientious care and prayer about the Spirit's past and promised achievements that glorify the Father and the Son.

So among the signs that the Spirit is being taken seriously will be

- *Christians conscientiously pursuing personal holiness*, practicing the disciplines of discipleship and making full use of the means of grace and growth (Bible reading, daily prayer, regular fellowship, active worship and witness, sharing in Holy Communion, and so on);
- *Christians conscientiously seeking congregational renewal*, in worship, fellowship, maturity, and outreach, with pastor and people collaborating to ensure that all minister and are ministered to with the gifts for service that the Holy Spirit has given;
- *Christians conscientiously studying and adhering to sound doctrine*, because it is the truth that the Spirit teaches in and from Scripture that is the means through which he feeds and brings health and strength to believers' hearts;
- *Christians conscientiously working and praying for the spread of the gospel*, and the extension of Christ's kingdom throughout the world—the grand project that the Spirit has been given to energize (see John 16:7–11);
- *Christians conscientiously trusting, loving, adoring, thanking, praising, and aiming to please the Lord Jesus Christ*, their Savior and friend, whom the Spirit is with us and in us to glorify (John 16:14).

Quietly and thoughtfully, now, let us ask ourselves directly: How seriously do we take the Holy Spirit? And how seriously are we going to take him from now on?

QUESTIONS FOR STUDY AND DISCUSSION
1. Do you agree that Anglicans generally, and present-day evangelicals generally, do not take the Holy Spirit seriously? Why, or why not?
2. Would you say that your own local church honors the Holy Spirit? Do you see any features of its life as obstructing the Spirit's work?
3. Do you endorse the account of the Holy Spirit's ministry to individuals that is set forth in these pages? If not, why not?

4. Do you accept this chapter's analysis of the Holy Spirit's ministry in the church? Do you see reason to add to it?

5. What seem to you to be the key elements of (a) personal renewal and (b) congregational renewal?

6. How may you know you have received and are indwelt by the Holy Spirit?

7. What do you see as the marks of personal holiness?

7

TAKING BAPTISM
SERIOUSLY

First, let us get clear as to what we are talking about.

BAPTISMAL BASICS

At the close of his ministry on earth, Jesus Christ our Lord pre-scribed two rites that his disciples were to maintain on a permanent basis after he had left them.

Number one has the form of a celebratory meal and was actu-ally instituted in the course of a Jewish Passover feast. It is called the Lord's Supper, or the Eucharist or the Holy Communion, and is to be regularly repeated. Right from the start the apostolic communi-ties seem to have celebrated it every Lord's Day (Sunday, that is), and at other times too when believers were together in worship (see Acts 2:42, 46; 20:7, 11; 1 Cor. 11:20–34).

Number two, which the risen Jesus included in his Great Commission to his apostles, has the symbolic form of a complete, comprehensive body wash. The Savior prescribed distinctive word-ing ("in the name of the Father and of the Son and of the Holy Spirit") to go with it, but the action itself was already in use as part of the process of receiving non-Jewish proselytes—converts, we should say—into the Jewish community. Also, John the Baptist, Jesus's cousin, had earlier imposed baptism as a token of response to his ministry—a sign, that is, of full-scale personal repentance and forsaking of known sin in preparation for the imminent appear-ance of the Messiah. *Baptism*, a term taken from Greek that means "washing," was already the established name for the procedure; the person administering it was called the baptizer; and in Jesus's day its symbolism of one being cleansed from present defilement in order to make a wholly new start in life was undisputedly understood.

The essence of baptism in practice seems to have been that its subjects were brought to water and then either literally submerged for a moment or metaphorically immersed by having water poured over their head as they stood in or by the water, upright. Whether both methods had an equal place in Jewish practice or in John's ministry, whether one was standard rather than the other, and whether Jesus specified one of these methods, we are nowhere told, nor does it seem to matter. In both usages, the symbolism of first going under water as a sign of saying good-bye to the style of life one is renouncing and then coming up from under as a sign of starting a new life pattern is clearly expressed, and that evidently is what is important. The washing symbolism shows that this commitment is conceived within the frame of an absolution from the past that sets one free for the new beginning. The rite is thus one of termination, initiation, and commencement. In the nature of the case, therefore, it should only ever be administered to a person once.

The fact that Jesus commanded these two rites shows that for him they were important. Evidently he saw them as a pair designating the Christian life first in its beginning and then in its continuance. As he presented them to the disciples, both, as we shall see, point to, celebrate, and serve to solidify the unique Spirit-and-faith bond with himself that is the believer's umbilical cord, so to speak, linking him or her with the life in Christ that begins here and is enjoyed in its fullness hereafter. Union and communion—intentional and experiential fellowship, that is—with the risen, reigning Christ, who is our sin-bearing Redeemer, sovereign Lord, friend and brother, help and hope, and with his Father, who is our heavenly Father by grace and adoption, is the essence of true Christianity. And it is this supernatural life, based on God's precious promises and ongoing love, and sustained in us by the Holy Spirit, that these two ritual actions signify, symbolize, and seal.

Taking its cue from Christ, the Christian church has always seen baptism and the Supper as matters of major concern and has developed three distinct ways of referring to them, each of which highlights an essential point about them.

First, the earliest postapostolic theology, like the New Testament, was written in Greek, the Roman Empire's common language, and Greek theology called these rituals *mustēria* (mysteries). The use of this word frames everything to which it applies with two thoughts: that this is knowable only by revelation, and that this is knowable only up to a point, for there is more to it than our finite minds can grasp. Here, both rites indicate the revealed reality of the God who is *there*, and the Christ who is *there*, and the heaven that is *there*, and the new life that is *there*—realities that, though invisible, are eternal; realities that the gospel message calls us to recognize and interact with; and realities to which our two rites are God-given signposts, both invoking the certainty of sense experience to assure us of the realities that correspond.

The answer to question 75 in the Heidelberg Catechism, a classic Reformation document, models for us the thinking that this should evoke within us in the case of the Lord's Supper.

> Christ has commanded me . . . to eat of this broken bread and drink of this cup in memory of him, and thereby has given assurance: first, that his body was . . . broken on the cross for me, and his blood shed for me, as sure as I see with my eyes the bread . . . and the cup . . . ; and, further, that with his crucified body and shed blood he himself feeds and nourishes my soul to eternal life, as sure as I take and taste the bread and cup.

As sure as is the key phrase here, the hinge phrase, we might say, on which the thought turns. So we may say that in thus ministering assurance the Supper truly functions on the principle that seeing is believing—in other words, that contemplating and actually consuming the sign confirms confidence that one is sharing in the thing signified. And with baptism it is similar: remembering, or being reminded of, one's baptism as a fact of one's past confirms the believer's certainty of being dead and risen with Christ in the present, and hence of being called here and now to live out the new life that God has imparted, making a difference in the world by being different from the world—a matter about which we shall have more to say in due course. In this way the two rites, viewed as *mysteries*, visible disclosures of God's saving work through Christ both past and present, accentuate their recipients' *assurance* that God has his grip on their lives.

Second, from early on, the Latin-speaking churches of the Western Roman Empire called these rites *sacraments*, the commonest label for them today. *Sacramentum* was a word borrowed from the army, where it signified the soldier's solemn oath pledging full loyalty to the Roman emperor, under whose banner he was enlisting. When Christians took the word over, the analogy shifted; the oath was now understood to be God's, a promise guaranteeing salvation to everyone who receives Jesus Christ as Savior and Lord, professes penitent faith, and commits to be fully faithful to God throughout life. This profession, though vital in itself, was seen as responsive and therefore derivative, and thus of secondary importance compared to God's own pledge.

So Article 25 of the Thirty-Nine, the sixteenth-century Anglican declaration of faith, says: "Sacraments ordained of Christ be not only badges or tokens of Christian men's profession, but *rather* they be certain sure witnesses, and effectual signs of grace . . . by the which [God] doth work invisibly in us, and doth not only quicken, but also strengthen and confirm our Faith in him." *Rather* is the word here that indicates primacy of importance.

And then Article 27, applying the above with Anabaptist sects in view, affirms:

Baptism is not only a sign of profession, and mark of difference, whereby Christian men are discerned from others . . . but
it is also a sign of Regeneration or New-Birth, whereby, as by
an *instrument*, they that receive Baptism *rightly* are *grafted* into
the Church; the promises of forgiveness of sin, and of our adoption to be the sons of God by the Holy Ghost, are visibly *signed
and sealed*, Faith is confirmed, and Grace increased by virtue of
prayer unto God. (Emphasis added.)

Note here the legal background being drawn on, which is often
overlooked. A *seal*, as in Paul's writings and in legal dealings today,
is a solemn confirmation of the authenticity and binding force of a
stated promise. An *instrument*, here as in many sixteenth-century
documents, is not a tool or piece of apparatus, as we twenty-first-
century readers might suppose, but a legal document, a deed of
conveyance, establishing someone's right to possess or privilege to
enjoy some specified benefit (in this case, a sharing in the authentic life of union with God that belongs to the real church, pictured
here horticulturally as an *ingrafting*, on the model of Paul's image in
Rom. 11:17–24). Note too that *rightly* (*rectē* in the definitive Latin
version) means, not "with ritual correctness," but "as one should"
in personal terms. The 1604 addition to Cranmer's Prayer Book
Catechism, still part of the 1662 Prayer Book, explains:

Q. What is required of persons to be baptized?
A. Repentance, whereby they forsake sin; and Faith, whereby
they stedfastly believe the promises of God made to them in
that Sacrament.

Q. Why then are Infants baptized, when by reason of their ten-
der age they cannot perform them [i.e., cannot yet repent and
believe]?
A. Because they promise them both by their Sureties [i.e., god-
parents, parents, sponsors]; which promise, when they come
to age, themselves are bound to perform.

Thus the language of *sacraments* highlights and guarantees God's promise of saving action for the future, linking this with the responsive promise of a life of repentance and faith that individuals are required to make at their baptism and renew every time they come to the Lord's Table.

Third, over the centuries the baptism of infants as a name-giving routine, followed in due course by passive, uncomprehending, noncommunicating attendance at the Lord's Supper, now renamed the Mass, became standard throughout the Western world. The need for the responsive commitment of faith and repentance was lost sight of, and the idea spread that both sacraments automatically conveyed the blessing they signified, simply by virtue of being correctly administered. Reacting against this superstitious sacramentalism, some Protestants dropped the word *sacraments* in favor of *ordinances*, sometimes expanding it to *covenanting ordinances*.

Theologically, there is gain here, for *ordinances* proclaims the reality of divine command, and *covenanting* goes to the very heart of what the rites signify. A covenant in Scripture is a comprehensive mutual promise and bond of goodwill and loyalty between two parties. The generic formula is, "I am yours and you are mine," and among human relationships, the prime example is marriage. Jesus spoke of the cup of wine at the Supper as "the new *covenant* in my blood," harking back to Jeremiah's prophecy in 31:31–34 and pointing forward to his substitutionary sacrifice for sins, shortly to take place. And God had said to Abraham long before, when instituting the initiatory rite that was baptism's predecessor, "This is my *covenant*, which you shall keep . . . : Every male among you shall be circumcised" (Gen. 17:10). The word *covenanting* thus speaks of the two-way street of pledged unity, fidelity, and tenacity—that is, love—that shapes the saving relationship between God the Father, the Son, and the Holy Spirit, and man the penitent believer. It is in these terms that God's bond with us and ours with him should finally be explained.

So far, we have bracketed baptism and the Lord's Supper together as a pair, which indeed they are. From now on, however, baptism will be our exclusive concern.

BAPTISMAL BEHAVIOR

This chapter reflects the conviction that Anglicans of all schools of thought, not to mention many other believers, have at least this in common: they do not take their baptism seriously. We may affirm that Baptism is important and give it a large place in our theology, but we do not think or pray or talk much about it as a defining factor in our Christian identity. Rarely do preachers highlight baptism (when, outside a baptism service, did you last hear a sermon on the subject?), and when they do they rarely get excited about it or press us to have it constantly before our minds. This seems particularly to be so in churches in which, as in my own, infant baptism is the rule. Baptisms are usually slated for Sundays, but in a way that makes them feel like perfunctory inserts into services that are otherwise dealing with more important business. An observer from another planet might well conclude that for present-day adults in the church, their baptism was merely a sideshow in the dim past, eminently forgettable, rather than an event of continuing center-stage significance for their Christian lives today.

Contrast with this the way in which in the second century, when Christianity was still technically illegal and open to official persecution at the local magistrate's whim, the baptism of converts was managed. It was programmed as one of the high spots of the Easter celebration, itself the highest spot of the church's year. At Easter, following three years of catechesis—graded instruction on the truths that Christians live by, and how one should live by them, and what current errors about faith and life must be discerned and avoided—one by one, the neophytes, having professed faith convincingly before the congregation, would be stripped naked, immersed three times, reclothed in white, which they were to wear for a complete week, welcomed into the congregation as full members at last, and admitted to the Lord's Table to share in their first Holy Communion. Three anointings of them with oil would punctuate the ceremony: the oil of exorcism, to banish malevolent spirits; the oil of thanksgiving, to celebrate the convert's new life in Christ; and a repeat of the oil of thanksgiving by the bishop, with prayer for the Holy Spirit's empowering throughout that new life. Big deal? Yes, surely, and an occasion that no neophyte was ever likely to forget. For that person, the ceremony would have had the same sort of significance as England's coronation service has for the royal person at its center. That service signalizes, celebrates, and expresses prayer for the new reign, just begun; it voices thanksgiving, joy, and hope as the nation embraces its new era, marked by this public recognizing and formal enthroning of its new monarch. It is a solemn landmark event, and so is baptism as described above.

Is it a great ceremonial occasion, then, that I aspire after when I speak of taking baptism seriously? No! And I ask the question only to dismiss that idea as decisively as I can. I have nothing against ceremonial, as long as it expresses and reinforces what is already in the heart; but it is what is in the heart that I am here concerned with, rather than anything else. You could have been baptized in the full second-century manner (it continued in essentially this form till at least the fifth century, and Eastern Orthodox baptism, for infants as well as adults, still embodies a good deal of it); it could now be one of your cherished memories, or cherished certainties about your upbringing; and still you might not be taking baptism seriously in biblical terms. Historically, baptism has been administered in many different situations, and in many different ways: to adults and young children and babes in arms; by pouring, sprinkling, and immersion; publicly, as part of a main Sunday service, or as an open-air occasion by a river, or by the sea; with some or all of the congregation present, or privately, as a family affair, either in church out of service times or in homes or hospitals; and amid a wide variety of theological beliefs as to what was actually taking place. But none of the methods, beliefs, or circumstances ensures that the baptism will be taken seriously, either by the witnesses or by the person being baptized.

So what do I mean by taking baptism seriously? My interest is in the difference that understanding our baptism should make to us, and I now offer a three-point biblical analysis that will, I believe, properly set this forth.

BAPTISMAL THEOLOGY

1. HOW BAPTISM IS PRESENTED IN JESUS'S GREAT COMMISSION

As Matthew reports it, what we call the Great Commission followed straight on from the risen Savior's momentous declaration, "All authority in heaven and on earth has been given to me." "Go therefore," he continued, "and make disciples of all nations, baptizing them in the name of the Father and of the Son and of the Holy Spirit, teaching them to observe all that I have commanded you" (Matt. 28:18–20).

"Make disciples" is a single Greek word, matching in meaning our own increasingly current use of *disciple* as an umbrella term for nurture. But what does that mean? Well, a disciple is essentially one who learns, that is, accepts instruction from somebody else, and a nurturer is one who gives the instruction needed for growth. A friend of mine wrote a book, boldly titled *Go Make Learners*, in which he argued that the central baptismal commitment is to spend one's life learning from Jesus through his teaching servants, as the apostles themselves had spent their three previous years learning from Jesus in the flesh; and that this commitment explains why, in Christianity's earliest days as recorded in Acts, those who professed faith in Christ were baptized immediately, rather than being made to wait for further instruction about discipleship before thus displaying their new allegiance. I think he was right on both counts. Baptism was then to be the converts' first step in the process of being discipled, as Jesus's own words ("make disciples . . . baptizing them . . . teaching them . . .") seem naturally to indicate and recommend.

But before being a response to Christ from the one being baptized, baptism should be seen as an embodied divine promise that is at the same time a call and a claim from all three persons of the Trinity. The phrase "in the name of" does not mean "on behalf of" or "as the agent of" or "with the authority of," as is sometimes supposed. Literally, as the ESV margin shows, it is "*into* the name of," and it comes from Matthew's original world of law, banking, and business, where its context was transfer of ownership. We speak similarly when we deposit money or register property "in(to) the name" of someone else, who is to possess and use it henceforth. So, when the baptizer says that he baptizes "in the name of" the Father, the Son, and the Holy Spirit, what he is announcing is that the person being baptized is being made over—designated, consecrated, given up—to the Holy Three as his or her joint-owners, and so is being brought, as we might say, under new management. The blessings that this under-water-and-up-from-under ritual visibly signs and seals—that is, displays as really real and personally offered—are for those who thankfully embrace the fact that now they belong to the Father as his adopted children, to the Son as his purchased possession, and to the Holy Spirit as subjects for his ministry of transformation. This is baptism's *covenanting* aspect, for this is precisely what baptism declares.

2. HOW BAPTISM IS WOVEN INTO PAUL'S ACCOUNT OF OUR UNION WITH CHRIST

When Paul, having triumphantly affirmed that the reign of God's grace overcomes the reign of sin and death, asks, are we to continue in sin so that grace may abound?, his explosive negative answer involves baptism, as demonstrating our union with Christ in his death and resurrection.

Do you not know that all of us who have been baptized into Christ Jesus were baptized into his death? We were buried therefore with him by baptism into death, in order that, just as Christ was raised from the dead by the glory of the Father, we too might walk in newness of life. (Rom. 6:3–4)

In Colossians he speaks to his Christian readers (strangers to him, as were the Romans) as those who had undergone what he calls a spiritual circumcision by means of this union.

In him [Christ] also you were circumcised with a circumcision made without hands, by putting off the body of the flesh, by the circumcision of Christ, having been buried with him in baptism, in which you were also raised with him through faith in the powerful working of God, who raised him from the dead. And you, who were dead in your trespasses and the uncircumcision of your flesh, God made alive together with him, having forgiven us all our trespasses. (Col. 2:11–13)

In both passages he appeals to the under-and-up ritual as representing the two aspects of our union with Christ, the deepest dimensions of our saving and eternal relationship with him.

Paul's understanding and exposition of salvation—"in and through Christ," as we regularly say—involves him in constant oscillation between two thoughts that, though inseparably connected, cannot be reduced to one. This to-and-fro mental movement, without which the fullness of salvation could not be expressed, is marked by Paul's use of prepositions, in the following manners:

When the apostle focuses on the new relation to God that the gospel proclaims—reconciliation and justification, pardon and peace, forgiveness and adoption—he speaks of these things as becoming reality for us *through* and *on account of* (*dia*) our Lord Jesus Christ, who died for us—that is, *on our behalf* (*hyper*, e.g., Rom. 5:6–8; Gal. 3:13)—and then rose, returned to glory, reigns now, and will one day return to earth to raise us if we have died, or to transform us if we are still living, for our final blessing and everlasting enrichment. What Paul is after in this is a clearheaded recognition that formerly, when we existed without Christ, we were ruined, guilty, and lost, and that every element of the salvation we now and will forever enjoy we owe to him.

When however Paul speaks directly of the Christian's new life according to the gospel, he always presents it as life *in* (*en*) Christ (101 times, no less)—that is, life lived in connection and union with Christ—and as life *with* (*meta*) Christ (sixteen times)—that is, life lived in conjunction and communion with Christ. What Paul seeks to induce here is a clearheaded recognition that it is the risen, reigning, accessible, active Christ, now with us and within us in the power of his resurrection life through the Holy Spirit, who has made us into what we now are, so different from what we used to be, and who continues remaking us, rendering our character more and more like his own. Paul wants us to know what has happened to us through our faith-union with Christ: namely, that within our unchanged personal identity, the power that made the world has made us into new creations (2 Cor. 5:17), terminating our old, self-centered, naturally sinful mode of existence and, to borrow again Paul's elegant horticultural image, grafting and implanting us into our risen Lord—plugging us into him, as we might less elegantly put it—with new desires, new powers, and new joys directly resulting. In terms of Paul's spiritual ontology, which tells us how God who brought about this change sees and knows his own handiwork, we have been co-crucified and co-resurrected with and in Christ (see Gal. 2:20; Eph. 2:5–6; Col. 2:11–13).

This change is precisely what the under-and-up ritual of baptism symbolizes; so this is the *Christ-centered* aspect of the sacrament.

3. HOW BAPTISM RELATES TO THE CHURCH

Integral to Paul's gospel is an account of the church, and basic to this, constantly implicit if nowhere explicit, is the distinction between the universal church and the local church. The universal church is the one worldwide fellowship of believers in Christ as such, and the local church is the particular band of believers who meet and organize themselves in a particular place and in a particular way in order to live out together the true churchly behavior pattern and thus to be sample, specimen, and demonstration in miniature of the organic life of the church universal. That church Paul pictures as the one multinational, multicultural, global, worshipping, serving, loving, laboring, suffering, growing, outreaching body in which everyone is personally united to the Lord Jesus by the Holy Spirit, and of which the Lord Jesus is now the eternal Head.

The unity of that church, which follows from all its members being thus united to Christ, has what we may call a horizontal as well as a vertical dimension. Being linked with Christ, and thus committed to love and serve him as our loving Savior and Lord, all we who believe are also thereby linked with each other. Thus committed to love and serve him as our loving Savior and Lord, all we who believe are also thereby linked with each other and thus committed to love and serve each other as our brothers and sisters in the Lord's family. All three key images of the universal church in Ephesians are corporate images in this sense, namely, the building, body, and bride of Christ. Or think of a bicycle wheel: within its rim each spoke is separately and directly linked to the hub, and via the hub linked to all the other spokes, thus constituting a single functioning unit. It is in this way that Paul thinks of the church.

It should not surprise us, then, that Paul, clearly anxious that no local church should ever forget or fail to grasp what it really is and is really meant to be, opens his exposition of how the one church, made visible in the many churches, should "walk in a manner worthy of the calling to which you have been called," by listing seven components of the church's oneness in Christ. And in this list we find, after one body, one Spirit, one hope, one Lord, and one faith, and before the final item, one God and Father, "one baptism" (Eph. 4:1–6). What point about baptism is Paul making here? Peter O'Brien answers that question well. "There is only one baptism because there is one Lord Jesus Christ in whom believers are united, one body into which all Christians are incorporated. Those who have been baptized into Christ have put on Christ (Gal. 3:27)." Paul's overall teaching on baptism, O'Brien adds, "does not make sense unless the notion of spiritual union with Christ . . . is in view" (*Letter to the Ephesians* [Grand Rapids: Eerdmans; Leicester, UK: Apollos, 1999], 284). And spiritual union with Christ means incorporation into the one worldwide society that is his building, his body, and his bride; a society to which some fully belong, while others do not but remain outside it; a society which, in its overall visible aspect, no matter how much it is crisscrossed by internal division, has a single universal entry rite that all acknowledge, marking off all its adherents from all nonmembers—namely, Trinitarian baptism. This is the *church-centered* element of baptism's significance.

BAPTISM AND BABIES

Why adults who profess faith in Jesus Christ as their Savior, Lord, teacher, and leader should be baptized is now clear. Jesus himself directs that all such be given the sign, symbol, and seal of the eternal bond with himself, and with the Father and the Holy Spirit, that is now theirs. This is a means of grace to them, assuring them of the mercy that has embraced them and keeping them conscious of the reality and ramifications of union and communion with Christ. True, someone who has been baptized on profession of faith may yet prove not to be a genuine believer at all (see, e.g., Acts 8:13–34; 1 Cor. 10:1–12), but the discovery of a rotten apple need not negate the goodness of the good apples that surround it. But a question remains: Why baptize babies, who cannot understand any of these things? By what warrant do Anglican churches, and others with them, make infant baptism the rule? On what grounds can Article 27 affirm, as it does, "The baptism of young Children is in any wise to be retained in the Church, as most agreeable with the institution of Christ"? How can the fittingness of infant baptism be vindicated, when the New Testament neither clearly instances it nor clearly commands it?

The answer, in brief (whole books get written on this subject!), is that all through the Bible we see God treating parents and their dependent children as a single spiritual unit, involving the infants with their parents in the covenant community in a way similar to that in which the children of Canadian parents are in solidarity with them as junior Canadian citizens from the moment of their birth. As these junior Canadian citizens should be taught by their parents and other mentors to appreciate and in due course exercise their citizenship, so the children of Christians, having been publicly dedicated to God and publicly received into the church fellowship in which their parents already share, should then be brought up to enter consciously and wholeheartedly into the life in and with Christ that has thus been, symbolically and in sign form, made over to them. In other words, they should be led to personal faith in Christ. As Archbishop Ussher wrote long ago, I only "have the profit and benefit of them [the promises, rights, and privileges given me in baptism] when I come to understand what grant God in Baptism hath sealed unto me, and actually to lay hold upon it by faith." The Prayer Book directs that when baptized infants, now grown into young people, know the contents of the catechism and give credible evidence of having laid hold of God's grant by personal faith in Christ, they should be confirmed (that is, blessed by the bishop as the believers they now claim to be) and welcomed with all the congregation's other adult adherents to the Lord's Table.

BAPTISMAL LIVING

Few of us, I suspect (as said above), ever think about our baptism when it comes to shaping our lives, and certainly the attitudes and commitments that Christians should develop can be formed in us without our baptism entering our mind. Nonetheless, just as wearing the uniform helps members of the armed forces to remember that, being in the services now, their first loyalty is to their country, and their first task is to obey the orders of their superior officers, so remembering that we have been baptized helps us to keep our Christian commitment before us in sharp focus. Martin Luther tells us that in his frequent bouts with the Devil and what he saw as Devil-inspired temptations, he would often think *baptizatus sum* (I have been baptized), and this thought would keep him steady and on track. The same, surely, should be true of us. In particular, there are three principles of discipleship to Christ that the enemy of our souls constantly encourages us to forget, but remembering our baptism will help to keep vivid in our minds.

1. BAPTISM REMINDS US ABOUT OUR IDENTITY

Do we know, and do we remember, who we are?

Our identity is the shape of our conscious selfhood. It is formed by the impact on us of our relationships, our circumstances, and our success or otherwise in our creative endeavors, whatever these may be. The Christian's identity is to be formed by our relationship to Christ as our Savior, Lord, and God; our teacher, brother, and friend—that is, by the relationship into which baptism, as a sign and symbol, brings us. Looking up in adoration, looking ahead in anticipation of glory, and looking around in order to serve others in love for our Lord's sake must increasingly become the disciple's expression of his or her identity, and our baptism commits us to be disciples lifelong. As disciples, we are saved sinners of whom grace has laid hold, whom Jesus our Redeemer is now, shepherd-style, leading home; we are privileged persons, whose death-day will in truth be a third birthday, following on from our natural birth as babies and our new birth as believers. As each of our first two births led to a widening of experience and an increased measure of joy, so will our third. A Christian's death is promotion, not tragedy, however early in life it comes; mourners weep for themselves and those left behind, but not for the one who has gone ahead of us. D. L. Moody said memorably, "Some day they'll tell you Moody's dead. Don't you believe it! That day I'll be before the throne; I'll be more alive than I've ever been." As Christian poet Robert Browning wrote, "The best is yet to be"; and as Christian prose writer George MacDonald said, "If we knew what God knows about death, we would clap our hands." The life that awaits us will be better than anything we have experienced so far. Thinking of our baptism, which speaks of us following Christ through death into resurrection life, will keep these aspects of our Christian identity vivid in our hearts.

2. BAPTISM REMINDS US ABOUT OUR SANCTITY

Are we clear and do we bear in mind that God both calls us to and empowers us for holiness here and now?

To believers, baptism proclaims the supernatural reality of union with Christ in his death. This means that, though sin as an anti-God energy remains present in our system, its dominion over us is broken, so that we can effectively resist it in a way that previously we could not do. "We know that our old self was crucified with him in order that the body of sin might be brought to nothing, so that we would no longer be enslaved to sin" (Rom. 6:6, cf. vv. 2–3). Our co-resurrection with Christ, which our baptism also proclaims, then means that as "the life he lives he lives to God," "so also you must consider yourselves dead to sin and alive to God in Christ Jesus" (6:10–11). "Now that you have been set free from sin and become slaves of God, the fruit you get leads to sanctification and its end, eternal life" (6:22). So "present yourselves to God as those who have been brought from death to life, and your members to God as instruments for righteousness" (6:13). Our personal life has thus been supernaturalized. The risen Lord, our holy Head, and the indwelling Spirit, our holy enabler, lead us now into the disciplines of mortifying, that is, resisting and progressively killing, sin (see Rom. 8:13; Col. 3:5), and of developing and practicing the holy habits that God's law and Christ's example both prescribe (see Gal. 5:22–23; Eph. 4:20–5:2). Thinking of our baptism will keep our nose to this particular grindstone also.

3. BAPTISM REMINDS US ABOUT OUR LOYALTY

Is loyalty to our Lord Jesus Christ a driving force in our lives?

Loyalty is a blend of gratitude, admiration, a sense of indebtedness, and appreciation of ongoing love and care. Loyalty to Jesus Christ is basic to discipleship, and as the soldier's uniform is a public commitment to loyalty to the nation and its causes, so the knowledge that we have been baptized should weigh with us as our irrevocable commitment to Jesus Christ and his cause in the world. Uncompromising faithfulness to Jesus in opposing the world, the flesh, and the Devil, and in standing steady and strong for him in all situations, is what our baptism requires of us. Does this mean becoming countercultural? anticonformist? unpopular? viewed as a rebel? penalized for our faith? Sometimes, yes. This is par for the Christian course, as the New Testament makes very plain. But loyalty to Christ requires that we seek to make a difference by being different; and as in baptism the Father, the Son, and the Spirit pledge loyalty to us, so we the baptized must see ourselves as having pledged our loyalty to Christ categorically, without any ifs or buts, and as committed here and now to live out that loyalty every day of our lives. Our uniform, so to speak, has been given us and put on us, marking us out as, in the Prayer Book phrase, Christ's soldiers and servants; we wear it permanently, and must never in any way dishonor it. Remembering our baptism will constantly remind us that this is so.

So the question presses: how seriously do we take our baptism? Over to you, now, for your answer.

QUESTIONS FOR STUDY AND DISCUSSION

1. How much has your baptism meant to you over the years? How often has it been in your mind? What effect has it had in shaping your life?

2. What relation do you see between the rite of baptism and the Christian's personal freedom?

3. In what sense is a person's baptism his or her entry into the church?

4. How would you recommend that those baptized in infancy should be discipled?

5. "Remember always that Baptism represents unto us our profession; which is, to follow our Saviour Christ, and to be made like unto him; that as he died and rose again for us, so should we, who are baptized, die from sin, and rise again unto righteousness, continually mortifying all evil desires, and daily increasing in all virtue and godliness of living" (Baptismal Service, 1662 Book of Common Prayer). What impact does this statement make on you?

6. What, if anything, should a congregation do to maintain awareness of the significance of baptism?

8

TAKING THE LORD'S SUPPER SERIOUSLY

RECONNAISSANCE: WISDOM AND WEEDS

The launchpad for this chapter is my very uncomfortable suspicion that taking the Lord's Supper seriously is something that deep down most of us simply don't do—including, alas, many who have no idea that they fall short at this point.

Granted, we may belong to churches that include the Supper in their regular routine of worship, and we may attend and partake because we are expected to and know we should. But in honesty we must admit that we are really more interested in the sermon than in the sacrament. We feel the sermon is more important, we expect more from it, and we concentrate on it more intensively and brood more on it when the service is done. We are perhaps aware that long ago there were Christians who saw both the sermon and the Supper as of prime value and who made much of preparing for Holy Communion and practicing post-Communion devotions, but this knowledge leaves us unmoved. We do not imagine that such old-fashioned behavior has in it any wisdom for us today.

Why do we Protestants thus dumb down the Supper? Why do we take for granted, as we seem to do, that it is of secondary and minor importance? The trouble is, I suggest, that we have been shaped more than we know by a superficial and reactionary tradition that tells us there is wisdom in not making too much of the Supper (or Eucharist, or Mass, or Liturgy, or breaking of bread, or Holy Communion, or the Lord's Table, or whatever we are going to call it). This tradition, like so many traditions, is a recoil—in this case, a recoil from what we see, or think we see, or are told is there to be seen, in Roman Catholicism, Anglican Anglo-Catholicism, and Eastern Orthodoxy, each of which makes the Supper the central act of the church's worship, but (so we are assured) attaches misconceptions and superstitions to it and then (we are further assured) dumbs down preaching, so that the mistakes never get corrected.

Now this is an ignorant caricature, and my first move in this discussion must be to beg my readers to expel it from their minds, in whatever form it lies there and however deeply rooted it may currently be. As gardeners know to their cost, weeds choke the growth of healthy flowers; they flourish spontaneously where seeds carefully sown die almost before they have sprouted. And in the fallen human heart the story is similar. Prejudiced distortions and malicious fantasies luxuriate there, while sober truth has to struggle, and struggle hard, to get a look in. What we will be referring to as the Catholic heritage may slip up on specifics, but, as we shall see, it is basically more right than wrong, whereas the idea that in Christian worship this sacrament is of secondary importance is basically more wrong than right. I say this to clear the ground for thinking out the doctrine of the Holy Supper by the light of Scripture, which is the task we shall now tackle.

REALIZING THE REALITY OF GOD

When a topic becomes controversial and opinions about it divide, the first step in discussing it should always be to go back to the foundational points on which there remains agreement and try in the light of them to map out where, how, and why disagreement has come in. Doing this in the present case means letting the Bible lead us right back to God's purpose for human life when he created our race.

God made humankind, as he made angels, to live eternally in fellowship with him, loving him for his loveliness, adoring him for his wisdom, power, and beauty, and serving him gladly in any way he might ask. Within the good creativity (or, if you like, creative goodness) of this purpose, he showed his love of significant variety by doing something for us that he did not do for angels. He made us integrated compounds, psychophysical units: that is, as we might prefer to say, embodied souls, or, we could just as truly say, ensouled bodies—in other words, personal selves living in and through physical organisms. Then he set us to live a preparatory life, lower than the angels, the purpose of which was to make us ready, through leading us to make ourselves ready, for an endless transfigured life, higher than the angels, in a world to come. We were given bodies to live through so that we might experience and enjoy other people and things in a way that angels, being bodiless, cannot do. We humans are so made that our bodily experiences and enjoyments, like the abstract, evaluative, imaginative, and controlling notions that make up our thought life, should naturally and instinctively awaken an appreciative awareness of God as the source of everything that is worthwhile. They should also stir up in us a sense of gratitude to him for the gift of life as such, and for all within us that enriches it; that is to say, all our powers of perception through the senses and the mind, and the many good, great, and glorious perceptions that result. More than that, every element and event in our ongoing existence is intended to stir up desires for, and hopes of, more of the same, but in quality grander and more wonderful than any of our present enjoyments—desires and hopes that God plans to satisfy up to the limit in the world to come. Thus the physical world that we have been made to inhabit and the processes of body and mind whereby we appreciate it are meant to be means whereby God engages with us, revealing his reality to us and drawing the reality of worship out of us.

And when in redemptive contexts God designates material objects as spiritually significant signs, visible pointers to particular aspects of his invisible but potent action to bless us (in the Old Testament, circumcision and Passover; in the New Testament, baptism and the Lord's Supper), the same principle applies. Discerning the divine authenticity of the sign and its accompanying words, we are to tell ourselves that the spiritual blessings signified are as surely there for us as these visible tokens of them are. We are to recognize the goodness of God in providing for us both the blessings themselves and the assuring signs of their reality, and with confidence we are to move into communing with God on this basis, looking forward as we do so to the greater glories and joys to which the signs themselves are here and now pointing.

The time-honored way whereby the church expresses all this is that it speaks of the entire universe and its contents as *sacramental*, and of the significant signs as *sacraments*. Mainstream Christianity has for centuries used the words this way.

But we are running ahead of ourselves and must backtrack. Fast forward, now, from where we began. Sin came in at the start of human history and not only brought us all under God's punitive judgment, but also twisted our human nature out of shape, so that now our hearts have a built-in distaste for, and aversion to, heart godliness, and our natural sense of God's glory in the created order is blunted. But God has graciously implemented a saving strategy centering on the incarnation, life, death, resurrection, and dominion of the divine Son, for the forming by him through the Holy Spirit of a new humanity, the covenantal community called the church. And Christ has commanded observance of two rites as bonds of unity within that community. In them, material items—water in one case, bread and wine in the other—become significant signs of his own saving ministry to us who as believers engage in the ritual actions. Both actions symbolize the restoring, through Christ's reconciling sacrifice, of our relationship with the Father and the restoring, in Christ by the Holy Spirit, of our love for God and godliness, through the untwisting of our moral nature by sovereign regeneration. The one is a rite of cleansing and initiation (baptism), and the other a rite of sustenance and continuance (the Lord's Supper). It is the second of these that concerns us now, and our next move must be to review in detail the way that the New Testament presents it.

REVIEWING THE NEW TESTAMENT DATA

The symbolism of the Lord's Supper is that of the meal table where the food we need for life is regularly served. Bread and wine, staple items in a first-century Palestinian diet, were already on the table as part of the Passover meal when Jesus instituted the new rite. Matthew and Mark give almost identical accounts of how Jesus took bread and blessed it (that is, gave God thanks for it), then broke it in pieces and distributed it, saying, "This is my body." Next he took and blessed the wine cup and handed it to the disciples for all to drink, with the words, "This is my blood of the covenant, which is poured out for many"—and Matthew adds "for the forgiveness of sins" (Matt. 26:26–28; Mark 14:22–24). The shared bread and wine over which these words were spoken thereby became pledges of the reality, availability, and actual bestowal of the beneficial effects of the divine action to which the words referred; this was the holy use to which material foodstuffs were now being put. Luke reports Jesus's words as, "This is my body, which is given for you. Do this in remembrance of me." And then, "This cup that is poured out for you is in the new covenant in my blood" (Luke 22:19–20). Paul, relaying the wording that he received "from the Lord"—by which he meant, from the lips of the original apostles—adds to what we have in the Gospels: "Do this, as often as you drink it" (1 Cor. 11:25). So Jesus meant the rite to be repeated, just as ordinary meals are constantly repeated (for most Westerners, three times a day). Since Jesus had undoubtedly spoken in Aramaic, and what he said had at first been transmitted orally, it should not surprise us that these Greek renderings vary slightly, with some omitting wording that others include, and others including wording that some omit.

Three notes, now, on the meaning of these statements:

1. "Is," with predicates "my body" and "the new covenant in

my blood," must mean "represents" or "symbolizes"—not "constitutes." The idea that Jesus's words worked like a wizard's spell, changing bread, and perhaps wine too, whether through addition or transmutation, into something other than what they were, has had a good run for its money, but seems impossible, if only because Jesus himself as he spoke was still with them, personally unchanged. In fact, the reference to Jesus's body being given for the disciples points to his forthcoming sacrificial death on the cross. He had, of course, stated earlier that he came "to give his life a ransom for many" (Matt. 20:28; Mark 10:45).

2. "Blood of the covenant" echoes Moses's words as he threw sacrificial blood over the people at Sinai: "Behold the blood of the covenant that the LORD has made with you" (Ex. 24:8). The covenant was the imposed relationship whereby God declared himself to be Israel's God, and Israel to be his people. The "new" covenant (of which Luke and Paul speak), prophesied by Jeremiah and expounded in part in 2 Corinthians 3:5–18 and more fully in Hebrews 8:1–10:18, is an upgraded version of the original covenant in which Christ's once-for-all sacrifice for sin ends the repeated sacrifices of the Old Testament, and true holiness, motivational and behavioral, is imparted by the Holy Spirit.

3. The phrase "in remembrance of me" points to twofold action, both aspects being defined by faith-knowledge about "me"—Jesus himself. Deliberate remembering—calling him to mind; joyfully, adoringly, purposefully contemplating him; praising him and praying to him—is our action. Renewing our gratitude for grace, our confidence in forgiveness by grace, our hope of glory, and our strength for service all by the Holy Spirit is his action. Alive and with us now in resurrection power, he is the true minister each time the Supper is celebrated; we should think of the bread and wine as coming to us from his hand and as his guarantee to us that in love he will continue to nourish us spiritually forever.

In the course of correcting the Corinthians for their thoughtlessness about the meaning of the Supper, and their lawless, loveless behavior at it, as if it was some kind of wild picnic, Paul gives us what is in effect a mini-theology of this sacrament.

The objective significance. The symbolic routine of repeatedly sharing bread and wine made significant by Jesus's words witnesses to the two most far-reaching events in world history. One is past, namely, Jesus's self-sacrifice on the cross, which opened the gate to eternal life for all who believe; one is future, namely, Jesus's return for universal judgment and the remaking of the entire cosmos, at which time sacramental rites will be no more. "As often as you eat this bread and drink this cup, you proclaim the Lord's death until he comes" (1 Cor. 11:26). Because of the supreme significance of this symbolism, reverence at the table is a must.

The subjective significance. "The cup of blessing that we bless, is it not a participation in the blood of Christ? The bread that we break, is it not a participation in the body of Christ? Because there is one bread, we who are many are one body, for we all partake of the one bread" (1 Cor. 10:16–17). Participation means sharing in, assimilating, or being involved in something. Everyday eating and drinking brings bodily nourishment as our physical system assimilates the food. The ritual eating and drinking that Christ prescribed brings spiritual nourishment to us through unitive involvement with him in the shedding of his lifeblood and the giving of his body to be broken. We thus participate in the redemptive death that the words of Christ memorialize, that the actual eating and drinking symbolize, and that Paul affirms elsewhere as fact when he says that the believer has been crucified with Christ (Rom. 6:6; Gal. 2:20). And this is only half the story, for the symbolism is also of Christ feeding us to keep us in life. The life in question is his own risen life, into which he draws all believers in such a way that we become "one body"—that is, if we may put it so, one vital organism—in union with him. From this union, through the Holy Spirit, spiritual vitality flows: health and strength for devotion and service; inner resources of love, ability, and power that we continue to discover within ourselves throughout our lives.

When Jesus, the incarnate Son of God, instituted the Supper, he knew that he would shortly be killed. But he also knew that on the third day thereafter he would rise from the dead and in due course return to the glory that was his before and send the Holy Spirit to mediate knowledge of his presence and power to all who should call on his name, that is, pray to him with some awareness of who he is and what he has done. He had in fact spoken of all these things to his disciples. So clearly he meant the regularly repeated Supper to be an invigorating encounter between himself and each worshipper, and expectant reverence was to be the temper of the gathering as a whole, in contrast with the casual, self-indulgent disorder that prevailed at Corinth (1 Cor. 11:20–22). Lack of love and mutual disregard within the body of Christ are always an offense against Christ himself, the body's Head and life; but never more than at the Lord's Table. Hence Paul's startlingly strong words to the disorderly Corinthians:

> Whoever . . . eats the bread or drinks the cup of the Lord in an unworthy manner will be guilty concerning the body and blood of the Lord. . . . Anyone who eats and drinks without discerning the body [i.e., the meaning of the symbol of the broken body of Christ, or possibly the scandal involved in disrupting the fellowship of the church] eats and drinks judgment on himself. (1 Cor. 11:27, 29)

These are not words to forget in a hurry.

RECEIVING THE BREAD AND WINE

For the members of every Christian congregation to remember Christ together by sharing in this symbolic meal is something that he himself has directed us to do, as we have seen; and as with everything else that Jesus tells us to do, it is up to us to do it in the best way we can. The words instituting the sacrament have shown us that remembering our Lord should mean both calling to mind his sacrificial death for us and embracing his covenantal commitment to us. And the act of actually taking the food and drink as from him should express the renewal of our trust in him and our ongoing dependence on him as our Savior, Master, discipler, friend, and indeed, as Paul says in Colossians 3:4, our life itself. It is this many-sided relationship that we must seek to express in what we do at the Lord's Table.

Remembering Jesus, like remembering anyone else we want to honor, means in the first place centering our thoughts on him, his aims, his actions, and his involvements, and holding these realities steadily and admiringly before our minds. In everyday terms it is, we might say, a matter of looking his way, looking at him directly, and looking at what he himself looked at when he was on earth. And then (since he is now in truth risen, alive, and with us, and actually ministering to us through the hands and voices of the worship leaders), it is a matter of speaking to him in our hearts about the things we are remembering.

This communing in love can be circumscribed in four directions.

1. Look *up*. "Up" here signifies, of course, not distance from us ("up there") but dignity overshadowing us. Though Christ is close to us, he is in every sense above us, and our way of approaching him needs to reflect our awareness of this. We should look up to the Lord Jesus, God's incarnate Son, now enthroned at his Father's side, as our Redeemer-ruler, our sovereign Savior, the supplier and sustainer of our peace, love, joy, and strength, and as the sender of the Holy Spirit to generate within us, in union with himself, the fullness of our newness of life. We should look up to Jesus the Mediator with awe and gladness that he has brought us into his Father's family and is here and now feeding us in a way that supernaturalizes our lives, and we should honor him for it with our praise and our thanks.

2. Look *back*. We should contemplate Calvary and all that it meant for us in terms of sin's penalty paid; reconciliation with the Father achieved; forgiveness made available for believers, and

justification and adoption by God made real for them; permanent security with God guaranteed to them; Satan decisively defeated; and the foundation laid for the full-scale reintegration in due course, through and under Christ, of this entire sin-scarred, sin-marred universe. Christ's transcendent achievement by his death on the cross must ever be central in our remembrance of and communion with him who is now our risen Lord and our true host at his table. "Far be it from me to boast except in the cross of our Lord Jesus Christ," wrote Paul (Gal. 6:14). Glorying in the cross, as Paul gloried in it, should be part of each Christian's mental and spiritual exercise as we come to receive the bread and wine.

Here it helps to recall the significance of Israel's Passover, in the course of which Jesus instituted the Supper. Scripture tells us that this annual event began as a divinely prescribed meal preparing for the deliverance of the community from Egyptian enslavement. It was two things together. It was, first, a shielding of Israel from the judgment of the tenth plague, in which all Egypt's firstborn died. The shielding was achieved by smearing the lamb's blood on the lintel and doorposts of each home. "When I see the blood, I will pass over you," the Lord said (Ex. 12:7, 12–13, esp. 13). In this, substitutionary atoning sacrifice was evidently being foreshadowed. And, second, the meal was given a form that spoke of hurried preparations for departure. "With unleavened bread and bitter herbs they shall eat it. . . . let none of it remain until the morning . . . . In this manner you shall eat it: with your belt fastened, your sandals on your feet, and your staff in your hand. And you shall eat it in haste" (12:8–11). Egypt's exit door would shortly be opened, and Israel must be ready to leave. Liberation from sin's dominion through the cross, the spiritual counterpart of Israel's earthly redemption, is being clearly anticipated here. Thoughts of all this will fitly enter into the look back in our devotional meditations as we come to the table of the Lord.

3. Look *ahead*. "As often as you eat this bread and drink the

cup, you proclaim the Lord's death until he comes" (1 Cor. 11:26). Christ comes, quite literally, to take every believer home, either at his future public coming for judgment, which Paul has in view here, or (as has been the case for every believer so far, and will continue to be till that momentous event) by personal self-disclosure to us at the point of our death. "I go," Jesus said, "to prepare a place for you . . . , I will come again and will take you to myself, that where I am you may be also" (John 14:2–3). This promise will be fulfilled, one way or the other, to all of us.

Courting couples, and married couples too, find great delight in phone conversations when they are away from each other, but the delight is greater when they are together, looking at and able to touch each other as they speak. Similarly, communion with the Father and the Son in prayer now will bring joy, but the joy will be greater in heaven, where each of us will simultaneously receive Jesus's full attention (being God, he is able to manage that, and indeed already does), and we shall see his face, and our fellowship of love with him will be unimaginably close and rich. At the Communion table, we should be looking forward to this and, in our hearts, telling our Savior that we are doing so.

4. Look *around*. We who believe are limbs or units or, as the KJV has it, members of the spiritual body of Christ, which is the church viewed, as it were, from the inside and known by the way it works. Our Christian life as church people is meant to be a life of constant loving service, both to fellow-Christians and to needy people, individuals and communities, that are outside the circle of faith. Our service is to be shaped and measured by the way in which the real needs of real people present themselves: Jesus's story of the Good Samaritan shows this. So as we share in the Supper, we should be asking ourselves, and asking the Lord Jesus to show us, what human needs we should devote ourselves to serving once our Eucharistic service is over and we have scattered back into the wider world. We would mar our professed discipleship badly, turning it

into formality, hypocrisy, and radical unreality, should we fail to reconsecrate ourselves at each Communion service to serve the needy, for in that failure we would be declining to love our neighbors as we love ourselves.

If these are the thoughts and concerns that should fill our minds as we come to the Lord's Table, we can now see the point of Paul's admonition, "Let a person examine himself, then, and so eat of the bread and drink of the cup" (1 Cor. 11:28). It is not just that we should not be thoughtlessly casual and disorderly, as the Corinthians were; it is rather that when we come to the holy table, we need to be reverent and properly prepared to focus on Christ our Lord. We need to be honest and penitent about ways in which we have come short of faithfulness and love to Christ and Christians. We need to ask the Lord for any new orders he has for us, and for new strength to do better the things we already know we have to do. And we need to express gratitude for grace received just as heartily as we can.

Worship patterns at the table vary widely. A common formula, following ministry of the gospel word in some form, consists of a hymn, a prayer for spiritual realism, a reciting of the words of institution, distribution of the elements, and a closing prayer of congregational thanksgiving, consecration, and dismissal. The historic Anglican Prayer Book liturgy, dating in essence from 1552, works up to the distribution with particular power by a dramatic sequence of the three key themes: sin, grace, and faith. Sin is articulated in a poignant congregational confession expressing penitence and pleading for forgiveness. Grace is articulated by a proclamatory prayer for mercy uttered by the minister and followed by "comfortable [i.e., encouraging, reassuring] words"—four New Testament quotations (Matt. 11:28; John 3:16; 1 Tim. 1:15; 1 John 2:1–2) declaring the saving mercy of the Father and the Son. Then faith is articulated in an outburst of thankful adoration, after which comes the sacrament, confirming and applying to each person the saving work of Christ that has just been celebrated.

RABBIT TRAIL: THE PROBLEM OF PRESENCE

The angle of our exposition so far has been devotional and practical, and it would be wrong to round it off by lapsing into jarring controversy. But something should be said before we close about a notion that has been prominent in the mainstream of Christian thought throughout the two millennia of the church's life, yet seems to be neither biblically warranted nor devotionally fruitful. This is the notion of Christ being personally present in a unique way in the Eucharistic bread and wine once these have been consecrated for use in the Supper by a duly ordained bishop or presbyter.

The view in question affirms that, while the outward form of these foodstuffs remains unchanged, they have hereby become, literally and ontologically, Christ-carriers, by supernatural divine transmutation of their interior substance (Roman Catholic), or by Christ adding himself in a supernatural way to the bread and wine (Lutheran), or by a supernatural process that, though real, is entirely mysterious to us and must be acknowledged so (Eastern Orthodox and Anglo-Catholic). I am one who thinks that all forms of this idea of a special, somehow localized attachment of Christ's glorified being to Eucharistic bread and wine are mistaken, but it is not my present concern to argue that point. My purpose is to flag the idea's unhappy implication—that if the consecrated elements are unique because Christ is present in them in a unique and special way, and if Christ is received in unique fullness and with unique efficacy by partaking of them, as is regularly assumed, then Christ is neither so fully present nor so fully available anywhere else. To believe in this unique presence is likely to generate superstition about the Supper and to weaken the everyday exercise of faith in Christ.

The exponents of "real presence," as all forms of this view are labeled, base their belief on Jesus's words of institution ("This is my body . . . my blood"), supported by his earlier words in the Capernaum synagogue:

> I am the living bread that came down from heaven. If anyone eats of this bread, he will live forever. And the bread that I will give for the life of the world is my flesh. . . .
>
> Unless you eat the flesh of the Son of Man and drink his blood, you have no life in you. Whoever feeds on my flesh and drinks my blood has eternal life, and I will raise him up on the last day. For my flesh is true food, and my blood is true drink. (John 6:51–55)

But the thinking purported to find support in the words of institution is not cogent. As mentioned earlier, "is" in these words means representation, not identity. It is "is" as in the leader's words in the Jewish Passover today when he holds up the bread and says, "This is the bread of affliction which our fathers ate in the land of Egypt." "Is" here unambiguously means "represents." And when Jesus said that the way to consume him, the true Bread of Life, was to eat his flesh and drink his blood (which, granted, sounds shocking, as if indicating cannibalism), he was talking about the faith that looks steadily to him as our sin-bearing sacrifice and draws steadily on him to sustain the reality of our spiritual life. Says Calvin:

> It is a false interpretation to apply this passage to the Lord's Supper. . . . It would have been stupid and senseless to talk about the Lord's Supper before it had been instituted. Clearly, Christ is speaking here about the constant and ordinary eating of the "flesh" of Christ, which is done only by faith. (*John*, ed. Alister McGrath and J. I. Packer [Wheaton, IL: Crossway, 1994], 170)

Calvin is surely right. To point up Jesus's meaning when he speaks of gaining life by eating his flesh, four times over John employs the relatively unusual, very down-to-earth word *trōgō*, which carries overtones of champing jaws and nonstop chewing, like the English word *munch*; and he uses *trōgō* each time in the present tense, which implies continuous, ongoing action. The action relates not to the Lord's Supper as such, which, as Calvin points out, had not yet been instituted, but to that to which the Lord's Supper itself relates—namely, direct faith-communion with Christ through the Holy Spirit in response to his own words of promise and saving work.

The down side of "real presence" teaching is twofold. At the Supper itself it encourages what we may call frozen or mystical prayer, the prayer of thought suspended and the mind made blank while attention hovers in face of what we perceive to be simply beyond us. Healthier is the alternative sketched out above, prayer that reviews and responds to key truths, both indicative and imperative, that God has revealed for our learning and to guide our living. Also, as has been said already, the doctrine of Christ's "real presence" in the consecrated elements implies that under ordinary circumstances Christ is more remote and distant from us than he is at the Supper. And this thought, if entertained, is bound to cool the outgoing of our hearts to him in daily fellowship. Thus the truth that through the Holy Spirit Christ is always present to bless us in the full reality of all that he is will be overshadowed, if not indeed lost sight of altogether.

This is why I see "real presence" teaching, however reverent and well meant, as a rabbit trail, a track that looks clear but is ultimately off track. It does not deepen Eucharistic devotion as it believes itself to do, any more than it matches actual biblical teaching, but its tendency, at least, if not always its actual effect, is to hold its adherents back from the full-time, full-scale, full-throttle intimacy with the Lord Jesus into which the New Testament allures us.

What then should we say positively about the presence of Christ at the Supper? First, we need to be clear that the presence in question is the same presence that Jesus promised when, before his passion, he said, "Where two or three are gathered in my name, there am I among them" (Matt. 18:20), and when, following his resurrection, he told his disciples, "I am with you always, to the end of the age" (Matt. 28:20). It is the presence of the triumphant, sovereign Savior, who is *there* in terms of his objective omnipresence and *here* in terms of being always alongside each believer with a sustaining and nurturing purpose. Clarity requires us to say, then, that Christ is present *at*, rather than *in*, the Supper. Though not physical, his presence is personal and real in the sense of being a relational fact. Christ is present, not in the elements in any sense, but with his worshippers; and his presence is effected, not by the quasi-magic of ritual correctly performed by a permitted person, but by the power of the Holy Spirit, who indwells believers' hearts to mediate Christ's reality to them. It is not a passive but an active presence, known not by what it feels like (often it is, in any ordinary sense of the word, unfelt), but rather by what it does. For by it our risen Lord draws us close to himself and renews our assurance of possessing, either now or in days to come, all the good things that he died to secure for us. And then, as a good meal energizes the body, so our Savior energizes us for renewed ventures in faith and love, faithfulness and obedience, worship and service. This is what we who believe should seek when we come to the Supper, and if we do, then we shall surely find it.

REFLECTION AND REASSESSMENT

I said at the outset, provocatively perhaps, that with regard to the Supper we should discover that the Catholic heritage, taken as a whole, has been more right than wrong, whereas the evangelical heritage, taken as a whole, has often been more wrong than right. The time has come to try to make my bold words good, and to that end I offer the following conclusions to our study:

1. THE LORD'S SUPPER SHOULD BE CENTRAL IN THE CHURCH'S WORSHIP

In saying this, I do not mean the Lord's Supper without preaching, nor do I imply that the Supper is more significant than preaching the Word. Word and sacrament are linked, we might even say twinned, in the kind of worship I have in view. My point is as follows: Jesus directed his disciples to join in this memorial meal on a regular basis, and it is clear that right from the start they did. Lord's Day by Lord's Day, congregations met for the Supper, as in Roman Catholic and Eastern Orthodox churches they still do. In the medieval West, however, the liturgy, being in Latin, was not understood outside a narrow circle, and lay Communion at Mass (as the Supper was then called) largely faded away. And then, at the time of the Reformation, when attempts were being made to put things back in order, two unfortunate events helped to marginalize the Supper in church people's minds.

In Geneva, Calvin's plea for a weekly Lord's Supper was rejected officially. He had to settle for the sacrament once a month, while weekly preaching services came to constitute Genevan Sunday worship the rest of the time. And Geneva's example was influential all across Protestant western Europe. Then in England, though the authorized Prayer Book, shaped by Cranmer, required clergy to serve Communion each Sunday following the Bible service of Morning Prayer, it was legislated that adults must communicate three times a year: at Christmas, Easter, and Pentecost. The legal minimum became the conventional maximum; the propriety of infrequent Communion became a national assumption; and attending Holy Communion came to be thought of, not as a regular requirement entailed by one's churchly identity, but as a devotional option, a matter of personal discretion and individual decision as to whether or not one needed to do this. Here, too, was an unhappily influential example.

It is ironic that in the circles most directly overshadowed by Calvin and Cranmer, both of whom desired so strongly to make the Supper properly central once more, most was done to prevent this happening. But that was how things went and for the most part have gone since, and the evangelical world generally still needs to take the Reformers' point. Let it be said, however, loud and clear: the Supper, accompanied by preaching, is a divinely instituted church ordinance, and it ought to be the gathering point for every congregation each Lord's Day.

2. THE LORD'S SUPPER SHOULD HAVE A REGULAR PLACE IN PERSONAL DEVOTION

As was said above, we live in days in which the Supper has been widely downgraded from a primary church ordinance to a personal option of secondary importance. At such a time, it is up to each believer to form a personal rule as to how best to fit the Supper into the pattern of his or her regular devotional life, alongside Bible reading and prayer, the other devotional basics. It is not for me to propose a pattern, but only to say that there needs to be one, and to declare that only when the Supper is part of the pattern, with prayerful preparation and follow-up, is it being taken with proper seriousness. So my present task is ended, and I leave my readers to pursue this matter with God our Father and Jesus Christ, our Savior and our Lord. How serious do we propose to be henceforth in honoring Christ by the way we share in his Supper?

QUESTIONS FOR STUDY AND DISCUSSION

1. How do you understand the description of the Lord's Supper as a sacrament?
2. Do you agree that the Lord's Supper should be the principal service of worship in local churches each Lord's Day?
3. Do you attend services of Holy Communion regularly? If so, why? If not, why not? How do you think frequency of attendance should be determined?
4. How far do you agree with what is said in the text about the presence and action of our Lord Jesus Christ at the Supper?
5. How should you prepare to attend the Lord's Supper? How should you follow up your attendance?
6. How would you make fellowship in the body of Christ at Holy Communion services as real and meaningful as possible?

GENERAL INDEX

absolution, 73

Acts of the Apostles, 21

adiaphoron, 48

adoption, 156

agnosticism, 30

aliens and exiles, Christians as, 62

Anglican Church, 31, 94–98
    and Christian unity, 51–53, 66–67, 95
    confusion within, 47–48
    diocesan system, 65
    formularies, 19–20
    on the Holy Spirit, 108
    need for catechesis, 38
    neglect of doctrine in, 34
    urgency within, 15, 17
    worship, 72–73

Anglican Church in North America (ACNA), 102

Anglican Church of Canada (ACC), 31, 46, 47–48, 81–82, 84, 102, 104

Anglo-Catholics, 66, 81, 148, 159

Apostles' Creed, 35, 66

apostolicity, of the church, 92, 100

apostolic succession, 66, 96

Ash Wednesday, 73

assurance, 129–30

Athanasian Creed, 66

Augustine, 41, 76, 119

authority, 24

baptism, 127–44, 150
    and Christian identity, 142–43

and Christian unity, 59, 60

and church, 138–40

and holiness, 143–44

as rite of cleansing and initiation, 150

and union with Christ, 136–38

Basil of Caesarea, 41

believing, as two-toned reality, 19, 20, 43

Bible, 21–29
    authority of, 24, 40
    and Christian unity, 61–62
    and doctrine, 39–40
    ignorance of, 25
    inspiration of, 23, 40
    instrumentality of, 23
    metanarrative of, 74
    as revelatory book, 20
    as Word of God, 22

Bible reading, vanishing of, 21

biblical criticism, 30–31

bishops, 95–98

blood of the covenant, 152

body, church as, 59–60, 90–91, 122
    and the Lord's Supper, 153–54, 157

Book of Alternative Services (ACC), 31, 73

Book of Common Prayer
    American prayer book (1979), 31
    on baptism, 131, 141, 144
    on bishops, 97
    and Christian unity, 66, 71
    and historic faith, 31, 37

General Index

Irenaeus, 36

Jerome, 24
Jesus Christ
    death on cross, 153, 155
    as God incarnate, 12, 20, 27
    and the Holy Spirit, 114–15
    love for the church, 103
    mediatorial ministry of, 36
    prayer for Christian unity, 53–56
    presence in the Lord's Supper,
        161–62
    return of, 157
    as revelation of God, 12
    as Savior and Lord, 43–44
    work of, 39
John the Baptist, 70, 127
justification by grace through faith,
    43, 94, 156

koinonia, 64
Kuyper, Abraham, 111

Lambeth Conference [of 1998], 99
law, 28
Lewis, C. S., 29, 63, 119
liberal theology, 34, 37–38, 52, 66, 82
liberation, from sin's dominion, 156
local church, 93, 139
Lord's Supper, 65, 127, 128–29,
    147–64
    frequency of, 163–64
    and repentance, 72–73
    as rite of sustenance and continu-
        ance, 150
love, 13–14
    as active, 55
    and Christian unity, 62–63
    for God and neighbor, 46, 118
    of self, 76
loyalty to Jesus, and baptism, 144

lust, 29
Luther, Martin, 69, 142
Lutherans, 71, 159

MacDonald, George, 143
marriage, 29, 46
Middle Ages, 96
missional ministry, 55
modalism, 27
modern world, 25
Moody, D. L., 143
moralism, 109
moral law, 28
mortification, 119, 144
Muslims, 52

new birth, 117
new covenant, 22, 152
new creation, church as, 89
New Testament pastoral letters, 21
Nicene Creed, 39, 66, 91
Ninety-Five Theses (Luther), 69
nourishment, in the Lord's Supper,
    153

O'Brien, Peter, 140
Oden, Thomas, 39
Old and New Testaments, 22
Old Testament, canon of, 23–24
"Old West" churches, 18, 52, 80, 98
one, church as, 91
ordinances, 132
ordination, of practicing homosexu-
    als, 51–52
original sin, 76
orthodoxy, 11, 18, 54
orthopraxy, 11, 18
Owen, John, 111

panentheism, 67
pantheism, 67

SCRIPTURE INDEX

For more information about IVP
and our publications visit

www.ivpbooks.com

Get regular updates at **ivpbooks.com/signup**
Find us on **facebook.com/ivpbooks**
Follow us on **twitter.com/ivpbookcentre**

Inter-Varsity Press, a company limited by guarantee registered in England and Wales, number 05202650. Registered office IVP Bookcentre, Norton Street, Nottingham NG7 3HR, United Kingdom. Registered charity number 1105757.

Catechesis consists of intentional, orderly instruction in the truths by which Christians are called to live – a sort of discipleship in 'mere Christianity'.

The fact that catechesis has fallen out of the life and practice of many churches today is a major loss, leaving Christians undernourished and spiritually sluggish. Professor J. I. Packer responds that 'it is catechesis – vital ongoing teaching and discipling – that hits the bull's eye': it is of the utmost importance in developing a church that maintains orthodox beliefs.

Packer urges Christians to know their faith so that they can explain it to inquirers, sustain it against sceptics, and put it to work in evangelism, church fellowship, and the many forms of service – this is the Christian's business of taking God seriously.

'Dr Packer has the rare ability to deal with profound and basic spiritual truths in a practical and highly readable way.'
Billy Graham

J. I. Packer is Board of Governors' Professor of Theology at Regent College, Vancouver, and the author of numerous books, including Knowing God, Concise Theology, Keep in Step with the Spirit, A Passion for Holiness and Evangelism and the Sovereignty of God. He served as general editor for The Holy Bible: English Standard Version and as theological editor for the ESV Study Bible.

9 781844 746095
ISBN: 978-1-84474-609-5

ivp
Inter-Varsity Press
www.ivpbooks.com

Image: © iStockphoto   Design: Kev Jones